F Journey with the ATHERS

De La Salle House

The Word of God Throughout the Ages

New Testament
1

F Journey with the ATHERS

Commentaries on the Sunday Gospels

Year A

edited by
Edith Barnecut, O.S.B.

foreword by
John E. Rotelle, O.S.A.

New City Press

Published in the United States by New City Press
86 Mayflower Avenue, New Rochelle, New York 10801
©1992 New City Press, New York

Library of Congress Cataloging-in-Publication Data:

Journey with the Fathers : commentaries on the Sunday gospels, year A
/ edited by Edith Barnecut; foreword by John E. Rotelle.

Includes bibliographical references and indexes.
ISBN 1-56548-013-9 : $9.95
1. Church year—Prayer-books and devotions—English. 2. Bible.
N.T. Gospels—Commentaries. 3. Fathers of the church.
I. Barnecut, Edith.
BX2178.J68   1992
264'.34—dc20   92-20685

Printed in the United States of America

Contents

Editor's Note

This collection of homilies on the Sunday gospels and principal feasts which replace the Sunday celebration is largely a revision of that first published for the Benedictine Office of Vigils. Texts drawn from the patristic period, supplemented by some from later writers following the same tradition, are now offered to a wider public in a fresh format. The original introduction by the late Henry Ashworth, O.S.B., has been retained.

Most of the passages were chosen by Father Ashworth, after whose death the work was completed by the present editor with the assistance of John E. Rotelle, O.S.A. Many people helped with the translations, among whom Audrey Fellowes and Michaela Whitmore, O.S.B., deserve special mention. The final revisions were done by Anne Field, O.S.B., and the editor.

Heartfelt thanks are offered to all, but especially to Father Rotelle, who gave invaluable advice in the choice of readings, made the original publication possible, and arranged for the present series.

Stanbrook Abbey   *Edith Barnecut, O.S.B.*
Worcester, England

Foreword

Throughout the Christian centuries the Bible, especially the gospels, has inspired many volumes of sermons and commentaries. Those written in the early ages of the Church have a special value because of their formative influence on later theology and spirituality—the two were always wedded. It was for this reason that some of the early Christian writers came to be known as the "Fathers of the Church."

The esteem in which these early writings were held is shown by the great labor that was undertaken to copy them by hand so that they became familiar to scholars throughout the known world. Sermons preached by Saint Augustine of Hippo in North Africa in the fifth century were read by Saint Bede in England in the eighth. The invention of printing made possible an even wider circulation. Editions of individual Fathers began to appear in the seventeenth and eighteenth centuries, due chiefly to the scholarly work of the French Benedictine Congregation of Saint Maurus, known as "the Maurists." In the nineteenth century J.-P. Migne published his monumental Patrologia Graeco-Latina (85 volumes, expanded in later editions to 168 volumes), and Patrologia Latina (165 volumes, later expanded to 220 volumes). This work, superintended by the learned Benedictine J. B. Pitra, incorporated the earlier Maurist editions. It was followed by more critical editions as further ancient manuscripts came to light.

Meanwhile translations were being made, though these were mostly of the theological and philosophical works of the Fathers or Church writers, the sermons receiving less attention. Not all of these writings, even of the sermons, speak to people of our day. Many are too diffuse for modern taste, or deal with subjects which are no longer of current interest. To find the gems concealed in this huge mass of material requires great labor, but this was undertaken after the Second Vatican Council to produce the readings in the revised Liturgy of the Hours published in 1970 and later translated into the various languages. This put the choicest passages from our patristic heritage within reach of the general reader. It was quickly supplemented by other collections of patristic and modern readings, one such being the present series *Journey with the Fathers* which will deepen one's understanding of the gospels read at Mass on Sundays or feasts which replace a Sunday. It puts within reach of all some of the treasures of our Christian tradition.

I have no hesitation in recommending it to those who would welcome fresh light on the gospels, and renewed inspiration.

24 June 1992   *John E. Rotelle, O.S.A.*

Introduction

The liturgical year is an annual celebration of the paschal mystery. This annual reenacting of the mystery of our salvation contains some periods of special intensity and has many highlights, but it is still the celebration of the one and only mystery of our salvation. The annual, weekly, and daily celebrations of the paschal mystery in harmony with the rhythm of the liturgical year makes the mystery of salvation present. When the great historical events of the life of Christ are celebrated by means of the memorial, their saving power is made present and their significance is revealed.

Christian thought will never exhaust the mystery of Christ himself nor penetrate fully the depth of his work for our salvation. Nevertheless the passages in this volume offer the reader an authentic meditation on the mystery of our salvation, a meditation through the centuries by the best thinkers of the Church. They also afford a valid interpretation of the scriptures and their message. The scriptures are not a code of moral precepts or a collection of norms for worship. The gospel is the Good News of Salvation and the account of our Lord's saving acts.

It is the liturgy which still proclaims this Good News of salvation in the liturgical assembly. This proclamation produces its effects in the hearts of those who listen. It illuminates the mind and demands a personal response. The worshiping community has both a need and a duty to enter into a true and vital relationship with God. This relationship is entered into by listening to the word of God read in the assembly and to the commentary on it. It is a true dialogue, whereby God speaks to his people in the scriptures and in their explanation,[1] and his people reply to him through the responsories.[2]

At this point it may be convenient to consider briefly the delicate question of the role of tradition in the interpretaton of the scriptures. Monsignor Neophytus Edelby, titular Archbishop of Edessa, has convincingly demonstrated that in interpreting the scriptures account must be taken of the incarnation and of the mission of the Spirit. The Christian exegete needs to keep in mind that one's purpose is to understand scripture in the light of the risen Christ.[3] There is a close link between the Bible and liturgy. The scriptures are at once both a prophetic and liturgical reality. The proper medium for the testimony of the Holy Spirit to the incarnate Word is the liturgical assembly, especially the eucharistic assembly. It is precisely in reference to the liturgical assembly that the scriptures are to be explained.[4] This view is endorsed by Monsignor Edelby when he shows how the Eastern Churches consider scripture "as the consecration of the history of salvation under the species of the human word, but inseparable from the eucharistic consecration where the whole of history is recapitulated in the body of Christ."[5]

It is against this background that the whole corpus of patristic readings should be considered. This wide-ranging survey of patristic literature provides a source of continual reflection on the unfolding of God's plan of salvation. The Greek Fathers were accustomed to view the history of salvation as a whole. They start from a point where the Holy Spirit of God brings about God's saving events and creates a community to witness to these events which took place in their midst. The Old Testament is thus seen as a first revelation of God and his people.

The New Testament is considered as the supreme revelation, which brings God's saving events and his people to fulfillment once and for all in Christ. Finally the "last times" in which we live are thought of as the manifestation of the Holy Spirit, who insures the historical realization of the plan of salvation and makes present the power of the incarnate Word and his resurrection.[6] This conception of tradition and its transmission through the power of the Holy Spirit is essentially liturgical. In the pages of this patristic collection its progressive development may be observed under the typical themes of *prayer (lex orandi), dogma (lex credendi), and Christian life (lex vivendi).*

This is not the place for a detailed description of the authors included in this collection. They range from Clement of Alexandria at the end of the second century to Saint Thomas More in the sixteenth. In selecting these readings an attempt has been made to provide commentaries on the biblical passages they were to accompany. A second guiding principle was to select readings in tune with the themes of the various liturgical seasons.

In assessing the adequacy of this collection, two further considerations should be kept in mind: the role played by the Fathers in the development of theology, and their ecumenical importance.

The Importance of the Fathers to Theology

That the Fathers cannot be ignored without detriment to our understanding of God's purposes has been shown by Dr. Hanson, who says that it is an illusion to think "we can jump directly from the Bible or from the New Testament to the thought of the 19th or 20th century, easily ignoring the doctrinal development which took place immediately after the period covered by the New Testament . . . Consciously or unconsciously the vast majority of believing Christians of all traditions look at God and at Jesus Christ through the spectacles of Nicaea, and probably through those of Chalcedon as well."[7]

Yet we should not regard the age of the Fathers as a golden age of peace and harmony within the Church. It was in fact an age of confusion and agonized searching for truth; it was an age both of weakness and of fulfillment. Under the pressure of history, however, the Fathers built the foundations of theology. They saw that the Old Testament types had been fulfilled in Christ, in whom the human race has already reached its consummation. They saw that the incarnation was the fulfillment of the divine promises to Israel and of the longings of the whole human race.

The Importance of the Fathers to Ecumenism

As early as New Testament times disunity resulted from racial, cultural, and intellectual differences. In his first letter to the Corinthians Saint Paul reprimanded them for their divisions. Forty years later similar disputes led Saint Clement of Rome to write his own letter to the Corinthians, urging them to return to unity. Later, the Platonic and Stoic traditions gave rise to two different christologies within the Church, the one at Antioch, the other at Alexandria. These schools of theology became a source of disagreement and tension and finally divided the Church.[8] Such divisions, however, have been overcome in the past, and they can be overcome again.

13

Yet although the Fathers faced problems very similar to our own, it does not follow that we can go to them for ready-made solutions or for formulas that would heal our own divisions. To do so would answer our needs no better than would the adoption of the minimum theological agreement as a basis for reunion.[9]

Rather, we should look to the Fathers as to a common heritage, which "in spite of all the vicissitudes of history still pushes the divided communions toward each other and convinces them that, to adapt the words of Pascal, they would not be seeking unity if they had not in some sense already found it."[10]

Moreover, we may profitably read the works of the Fathers in order to become better acquainted with the spirit in which they met and solved their problems and healed their divisions. The concern here should be with their theology itself, not the way in which they expressed it. The theology of the Fathers was a theology of contemplation under the guidance of the Holy Spirit.[11] It was a theology they applied to daily life as they sought to resolve their difficulties.

For these reasons it may be hoped that this selection of readings from the Fathers will be of value in furthering the cause of ecumenism.

The Quest for God

The basis of monastic life, as understood by Saint Benedict, is a spirit of prayer and a desire for God. The means of attaining knowledge of God are the holy scriptures and the writings of the orthodox Fathers. In providing these tools Benedict was simply following tradition. Evagrius of Pontus (346-349) expressed the same truth when he affirmed that theology is a matter of prayer, not of philosophical training.[12] Until the twelfth century, theological teaching and study existed mainly in a monastic environment. Theology tended in consequence to be traditionalist, contemplative, and closely integrated with the liturgy. The monastic authors of the early Middle Ages represent in theology the stage between the patristic age and the scholastics, and therefore cannot be passed over in a collection such as this.[13] Their theology is the result of their method of reading the scriptures and the Fathers, a method linking the triad of *lectio divina, meditatio,* and *contemplatio.*

It will be seen that the emphasis in this collection is on the spiritual life, which Saint Gregory of Nyssa regards as an endless quest for God.[14] It is hoped that these readings will provide priests, religious, monks, and nuns and also the faithful at large with a means of entry into a world which will both deepen their knowledge of God and inspire them to strive for holiness: "For you have made us for yourself, and our heart is restless until it rests in you."[15]

Henry Ashworth, O.S.B.

Notes

1. See Sacred Congregation of Rites, instruction *Eucharisticum mysterium*, 25 May 1967, no. 55:AAS 59 (1967) 568-569.

2. See *Officium Divinum: Liturgia Horarum iuxta ritum Romanum* (Vatican City, 1972), Institutio generalis, nos. 169-171; Francois Louvel, O.P., "La Bible de la liturgie," *La Maison-Dieu* 129 (1977) 139-147.

3. See Monsignor Neophytus Edelby, "On Scripture and Tradition," *One in Christ* 1 (1965) 298-300.

4. See H. B. Meyer, "Schriftverstandnis und liturgie," *Zeitschrift fur katholische Theologie* 88 (1966) 163-184.

5. Monsignor Edelby, *op. cit.*, page 299.

6. See *ibid.*, pages 299-300.

7. R. P. C. Hanson, "The Age of the Fathers: its significance and limits," *Eastern Churchs Review* 2 (1968) 131.

8. Jean Danielou, Lecture given at the Fourth International Conference on Patristic Studies, Oxford, 1963.

9. See M. Van Parys, "Le rôle de la théologie patristique dans l'avenir de l'oecumenisme," *Irenikon* 44 (1971) 7-22.

10. Hanson, *op. cit.*, page 133.

11. See Van Parys, *op. cit.*, pages 17-22.

12. "If you are a theologian, you will pray truly; and if you pray truly, you are a theologian": Evagrius of Pontus, *De oratione* (formerly attributed to Nylus of Ancyra), chapter 60: PG 79, 1180.

13. See F. Vandenbroucke, O.S.B., "Sur la théologie de la liturgie," *Nouvelle Révue Théologique* 92 (1970) 138-139.

14. See Gregory of Nyssa, *In Cantica Canticorum* 5: PG 44, 873 - 876; *Contra Eunomium* 1: PG 45, 340.

15. Augustine, *Confessions* 1, 1.

First Sunday of Advent

Gospel: Matthew 24:37-44

Stay awake, you must be ready.

Commentary: Paschasius Radbertus

Watch, *for you do not know the day or the hour.* Like many other scriptural texts, this admonition is addressed to all of us, though it is formulated in such a way that it would seem to concern only Christ's immediate audience. We can all apply it to ourselves because the Last Day and the end of the world will come for each of us on the day we depart this present life. This means we must make sure we die in the state in which we wish to appear on the Day of Judgment. Bearing this in mind each of us should guard against being led astray and failing to keep watch, otherwise the day of the Lord's return may take us unawares. If the last day of our life finds us unprepared, then we shall be unprepared on that day also.

I do not for a moment believe the apostles expected the Lord to return in judgment during their own lifetime. All the same there can be no doubt that they took every care not to be drawn from the right path. They kept watch, observing the universal precepts their master had given to his disciples so as to be ready when he came again.

Consequently we must always be on the lookout for Christ's twofold coming, the one when we shall have to give an account of everything we have done, and the other when he comes day after day to stir our consciences. He comes to us now in order that his future coming may find us prepared. If my conscience is burdened with sin what good will it do me to know when the Day of Judgment will be? Unless the Lord comes to my soul beforehand and makes his home with me, unless Christ lives in me and speaks his word in my heart, it is useless for me to know if and when his coming will take place. Only if Christ is already living in me and I in him will it go well with me when he comes in judgment. If I have already died to the world and am able to say, *The world is crucified to me, and I to the world,* then, in a sense, his final coming is already present to me.

Consider also our Lord's warning: *Many will come in my name.* It is only the Antichrist and his members who, albeit falsely, claim the name of Christ, though they lack his works and his true doctrine and wisdom. You will never find the Lord in Scripture actually declaring, "I am the Christ." His teaching and miracles revealed it clearly enough, for the Father was at work in him. Louder than a thousand acclamations his teaching and mighty works proclaimed: "I am the Christ." And so whether or not you find him describing himself in so many words, the works of the Father and his own message of love declared what he was, whereas the false christs who possessed neither godly deeds nor holy doctrine loudly claimed to be what they were not.

(Commentary on Saint Matthew's Gospel
2, 24: PL 120, 799-800)

Paschasius Radbertus (c.785-860) was brought up by the nuns of Notre Dame at Soissons, after being left abandoned on their doorstep. He received the monastic habit at Corbie, and was the confidant of two successive abbots. On the death of Abbot Wala Paschasius himself became abbot, but he found the office uncongenial and resigned after seven years. He always refused to be raised to the priesthood. Paschasius, who was a prolific writer, is noted especially for the part he played in establishing the Catholic doctrine on the eucharist. He also wrote lengthy commentaries on Matthew and on the forty-fourth psalm.

Second Sunday of Advent

Gospel: Matthew 3:1-2

Repent, for the kingdom of God is at hand.

Commentary: Augustine

The gospel tells us that some people were rebuked by the Lord because, clever as they were at reading the face of the sky, they could not recognize the time for faith when the kingdom of heaven was at hand. It was the Jews who received this reprimand, but it has also come down to us. The Lord Jesus began his preaching of the gospel with the admonition: *Repent, for the kingdom of heaven is at hand.* His forerunner, John the Baptist, began his in the same way: *Repent,* he said, *for the kingdom of heaven is at hand.* Today, for those who will not repent at the approach of the kingdom of heaven, the reproof of the Lord Jesus is the same. As he points out himself, *You cannot expect to see the kingdom of heaven coming. The kingdom of heaven,* he says elsewhere, *is within you.*

Each of us would be wise therefore to take to heart the advice of his teacher, and not waste this present time. It is now that our Savior offers us his mercy; now, while he still spares the human race. Understand that it is in hope of our conversion that he spares us, for he desires no one's damnation. As for when the end of the world will be, that is God's concern. Now is the time for faith. Whether any of us here present will see the end of the world I know not; very likely none of us will. Even so, the time is very near for each of us, for we are mortal. There are hazards all around us. We should be in less danger from them were we made of glass. What is more fragile than a vessel of glass? And yet it can be kept safe and last indefinitely. Of course it is exposed to accidents, but it is not liable to old age and the suffering it brings. We therefore are the more frail and infirm. In our weakness we are haunted by fears of all the calamities that regularly befall the human race, and if no such calamity overtakes us, still, time marches on. We may evade the blows of fortune, but shall we evade death? We may escape perils from without but shall we escape what comes from within us? Now, suddenly, we may be attacked by any malady. And if we are spared? Even so, old age comes at last, and nothing will delay it.

(Sermon 109, 1: PL 38, 636)

Augustine (354-430) was born at Thagaste in Africa and received a Christian education, although he was not baptized until 387. In 391 he was ordained priest and in 395 he became coadjutor bishop to Valerius of Hippo, whom he succeeded in 396. Augustine's theology was formulated in the course of his struggle with three heresies: Manichaeism, Donatism, and Pelagianism. His writings are voluminous and his influence on subsequent theology immense. He molded the thought of the Middle Ages down to the thirteenth century. Yet he was above all a pastor and a great spiritual writer.

Third Sunday of Advent

Gospel: Matthew 11:2-11

Are you the one who is to come, or are we to look for someone else?

Commentary: Thomas of Villanova

The gospel narrative tells of a question which John the Baptist, who was in prison, put to the Lord through his disciples. *Are you the one who is to come, or are we to look for someone else?* John himself was in no doubt about the matter. Even from his mother's womb he had recognized Jesus, and at the Jordan he had borne his testimony; but he sent this embassy for two reasons.

In the first place, John wished to instruct his disciples. He knew that his own death was imminent and, like the good leader and teacher he was, he made provision for his disciples, to ensure that they would have a teacher and protector. He wanted to see them safe under Christ's wing and in his care.

John's second and paramount motive, however, was to draw attention to Christ. He knew that he had been sent to bear witness to Christ, and although he had given his testimony at the Jordan, few had accepted it. Knowing now that his death was near he devised a profitable and very prudent plan: he would put this question to Jesus publicly and thus bring him into the limelight, so that in replying to the question Jesus would at the same time bear witness about himself, and thereby reveal himself to the people. John knew that the Lord's reply was bound to be very fruitful, and events proved him right.

The disciples approached Jesus, and in front of the crowd put to him the same question which the Jews had put to John. Everyone eagerly awaited his reply, for there had already been a rumor among the people that he might indeed be the Messiah. The Lord gave no immediate answer, but delayed a little, and in their presence worked wonderful, mighty miracles. Then he invited them, *Go and report to*

John what you have heard. The blind are receiving their sight, the lame are walking, lepers are cleansed, the deaf hear, the dead rise again, and the good news is proclaimed to the poor. He did not give an answer to them in so many words, but pointed to his deeds, as much as to say, *"The works that I am doing are my witness.* These are the works I am performing; judge for yourself whether I am the Messiah." This was an admirable reply, for he not only claimed by means of his works that he was the Messiah; he also proved it.

Isaiah had uttered three prophecies about Christ. The first was this: *Then shall the eyes of the blind be opened, and the ears of the deaf unsealed, and the lame man will leap like a hart.* The second was, *The Spirit of the Lord is upon me . . . he has sent me to announce good tidings to the poor.* The third declared, *He will be a stone for stumbling over, and a rock of scandal as well, for both houses of Israel.* The Lord fulfilled these prophecies before their eyes, and implicitly quoted them in his reply: the first, by saying, *The blind are receiving their sight, the lame are walking . . . the deaf hear;* the second in his claim that the good news is proclaimed to the poor; and the third by saying, *Blessed is anyone who takes no offense at me.*

(Sermon 4 of the Second Sunday of Advent:
Opera Omnia, I, 80-81)

Thomas of Villanova (1486-1555) abandoned an academic career to become in 1516 an Augustinian friar. In 1533 while provincial he sent friars to the New World. After having declined the see of Granada, he was put under obedience to accept the archbishopric of Valencia which had been so neglected that he was excused from attending the Council of Trent. His time and money were devoted to the poor, the sick, and ransoming captives, so that he was called the Beggar Bishop, father of the poor. His many sermons had an influence on Spanish spiritual literature.

Fourth Sunday of Advent

Gospel: Matthew 1:18-24

Jesus was born of Mary, the betrothed of Joseph, a son of David.

Commentary: Bede

Matthew the evangelist gives us an account of the way in which the eternal Son of God, begotten before the world began, appeared in time as the Son of Man. His description is brief but absolutely true. By tracing the ancestry of our Lord and Savior Jesus Christ through the male line he brings it down from Abraham to Joseph, the husband of Mary. It is indeed fitting in every respect that when God decided to become incarnate for the sake of the whole human race none but a virgin should be his mother, and that, since a virgin was privileged to bring him into the world, she should bear no other son but the son who is God.

Behold, a virgin will conceive and bear a son, and he will be called Emmanuel, a name which means God-with-us. The name God-with-us, given to our Savior by the prophet, signifies that two natures are united in his one person. Before time began he was God, born of the Father, but in the fullness of time he became Emmanuel, God-with-us, in the womb of his mother, because when the Word was made flesh and lived among us he deigned to unite our frail human nature to his own person. Without ceasing to be what he had always been, he began in a wonderful fashion to be what we are, assuming our nature in such a way that he did not lose his own.

And so Mary gave birth to her firstborn son, the child of her own flesh and blood. She brought forth the God who had been born of God before creation began, and who, in his created humanity, rightfully surpassed the whole of creation. And Scripture says she named him Jesus.

Jesus, then, is the name of the Virgin's son. According to the angel's explanation, it means one who is to save his people from their sins. In doing so he will also deliver them from any defilement of mind and body they have incurred on account of their sins.

But the title "Christ" implies a priestly or royal dignity. In the Old Testament it was given to both priests and kings on account of the anointing with chrism or holy oil which they received. They prefigured the true king and high priest who, on coming into this world, was anointed with the oil of gladness above all his peers. From this anointing or chrismation he received the name of Christ, and those who share in the anointing which he himself bestows, that is the grace of the Spirit, are called Christians.

May Jesus Christ fulfill his saving task by saving us from our sins; may he discharge his priestly office by reconciling us to God the Father, and may he exercise his royal power by admitting us to his Father's kingdom, for he is our Lord and God, who lives and reigns with the Father and the Holy Spirit for ever and ever. Amen.

(Homily 5 on the Christmas Vigil: CCL 122, 32-36)

Bede (c.673-735), who received the title of Venerable less than a century after his death, was placed at the age of seven in the monastery of Wearmouth, then ruled by Saint Benet Biscop. From there he was sent to Jarrow, probably at the time of its foundation in about 681. At the age of 30 he was ordained priest. His whole life was devoted to the study of Scripture, to teaching, writing, and the prayer of the Divine Office. He was famous for his learning, although he never went beyond the bounds of his native Northumbria. Bede is best known for his historical works, which earned him the title "Father of English History." His Historia Ecclesiastica Gentis Anglorum is a primary source for early English history, especially valuable because of the care he took to give his authorities, and to separate historical fact from hearsay and tradition. In 1899 Bede was proclaimed a doctor of the Church.

Christmas

Gospel: Luke 2:1-14

Today a savior has been born for you.

Commentary: Theodotus of Ancyra

The Lord of all comes as a slave amidst poverty. The huntsman has no wish to startle his prey. Choosing for birthplace an unknown village in a remote province, he is born of a poor maiden and accepts all that poverty implies, for he hopes by stealth to ensnare and save us.

If he had been born to high rank and amidst luxury, unbelievers would have said the world had been transformed by wealth. If he had chosen as his birthplace the great city of Rome, they would have thought the transformation had been brought about by civil power. Suppose he had been the son of an emperor. They would have said: "How useful it is to be powerful!" Imagine him the son of a senator. It would have been: "Look what can be accomplished by legislation!"

But in fact, what did he do? He chose surroundings that were poor and simple, so ordinary as to be almost unnoticed, so that people would know it was the Godhead alone that had changed the world. This was his reason for choosing his mother from among the poor of a very poor country, and for becoming poor himself.

Let the manger teach you how poor the Lord was: he was laid in it because he had no bed to lie on. This lack of the necessaries of life was a most appropriate prophetic foreshadowing. He was laid in a manger to show that he would be the food even of the inarticulate. The Word of God drew to himself both the rich and the poor, both the eloquent and the slow of speech as he lay in the manger in poverty.

Do you not see how his lack of worldly goods was a prophecy and how his poverty, accepted for our sake, showed his accessibility to all? No one was afraid to approach Christ, overawed by his immense wealth; no one was kept from coming to him by the grandeur of his royal estate. No, he who was offering himself for the salvation of the world came as an ordinary worker.

The Word of God in a human body was laid in a manger, so that both the eloquent and the slow of speech would have courage to share in the food of salvation. Perhaps this is what the prophet foretold when he said, speaking of the mystery of the manager: The ox knows its owner and the ass its master's manger, but Israel does not know me; my people have not understood. He whose godhead made him rich became poor for our sake, so as to put salvation within the reach of everyone. This was the teaching of Saint Paul when he said: He was rich, but for our sake he became poor, to make us rich through his poverty.

Who was rich, what was his wealth, and how did be become poor for our sake? Tell me, who was this possessor of great wealth who became a sharer in my poverty? Could he have been a mere man? If so he would never have been rich, for his parents were poor just as he was. Then who was this person possessed of great riches and what were the riches of him who became poor for our sake? Scripture says it is God who enriches his creatures. It must then have been God who became poor, who made his own the poverty of one who can be seen. His divinity made God rich, but he became poor for our sake.

(Homily 1 on Christmas: PG 77, 1360-1361)

Theodotus (c.446) was bishop of Ancyra, the modern Ankara. He was at first a friend of Nestorius, but became one of his most determined opponents. Because of the support he gave to Cyril of Alexandria at the Council of Ephesus (431), he was excommunicated by the Antiochene bishops at their synod at Tarsus in 432.

Holy Family

Gospel: Matthew 2:13-15.19-23

Take the child and his mother, and flee to Egypt.

Commentary: John Chrysostom

Today, as a firstborn son, Christ went down into Egypt to end the mourning its ancient bereavement had brought upon that land. Instead of plagues he brought joy, instead of night and darkness he gave the light of salvation.

Of old the river's water had been polluted by the untimely deaths of murdered infants. Therefore he who long ago had stained the waters red went down into Egypt and purified those waters by the power of the Holy Spirit, making them the source of salvation. When the Egyptians were afflicted they raged against God and denied him. Therefore he went down into Egypt, filled devout souls with the knowledge of God and made the river more productive of martyrs than it was of ears of grain.

What more shall I say of this mystery? I see a carpenter and a manger, an infant and swaddling clothes, a virgin giving birth without the necessaries of life; nothing but poverty and complete destitution. Have you ever seen wealth in such great penury? How could he who was rich have become, for our sake, so poor that he had neither bed nor bedding but was laid in a manger? O immeasurable wealth concealed in poverty! He lies in a manger, yet he rocks the whole world. He is bound with swaddling bands, yet he breaks the bonds of sin. Before he could speak he taught the wise men and converted them. What else can I say? Here is the newborn babe, wrapped in swaddling clothes and lying in a manger. With him are Mary, virgin and mother, and Joseph who was called his father.

Joseph was only betrothed to Mary when the Holy Spirit overshadowed her; so he was at a loss as to what he should call the child. While he was in this perplexity a message from heaven came to him by the voice of an angel: *Do not be afraid, Joseph. It is by the Holy Spirit that she has conceived this child.* In her virginity the Holy Spirit overshadowed her.

Why was Christ born of a virgin, and her virginity preserved inviolate? Because of old the devil had deceived the virgin Eve, Gabriel brought the Good News to the Virgin Mary. Having fallen into the trap, Eve spoke the word that led to death. Having received the good News, Mary gave birth to the incarnate Word who has brought us eternal life.

(Christmas Homily: PG 56, 392)

John Chrysostom (c.347-407) was born at Antioch and studied under Diodore of Tarsus, the leader of the Antiochene school of theology. After a period of great austerity as a hermit, he returned to Antioch where he was ordained deacon in 381 and priest in 386. From 386 to 397 it was his duty to preach in the principal church of the city, and his best homilies, which earned him the title "Chrysostomos" or "the golden-mouthed," were preached at this time. In 397 Chrysostom became patriarch of Constantinople, where his efforts to reform the court, clergy, and people led to his exile in 404 and finally to his death from the hardships imposed on him. Chrysostom stressed the divinity of Christ against the Arians and his full humanity against the Apollinarians, but he had no speculative bent. He was above all a pastor of souls, and was one of the most attractive personalities of the early Church.

Mary, Mother of God

Gospel: Luke 2:16-21

The shepherds found Mary and Joseph, and the infant lying in the crib. . . .
When the eighth day came, they gave him the name of Jesus.

Commentary: Guerric of Igny

One and unique was Mary's child, the only Son of his Father in heaven and the only son of his mother on earth. Mary alone was virgin-mother, and it is her glory to have borne the Father's only Son. But now she embraces that only son of hers in all his members. She is not ashamed to be called the mother of all those in whom she recognizes that Christ her Son has been or is on the point of being formed.

Our ancient mother Eve was more of a stepmother than a true mother, passing on to her children the sentence of death before bringing them into the light of day. Her name indeed means "mother of all the living," but she proved more truly to be the slayer of the living or the mother of the dying, since for her to give birth was to transmit death.

Eve being unable to respond faithfully to the meaning of her name, its mysterious import was fully expressed by Mary. Like the Church of which she is the model, Mary is the mother of all who are born again to new life. She is the mother of him who is the Life by which all things live; when she bore him, she gave new birth in a sense to all who were to live by his life.

Recognizing that by virtue of this mystery she is the mother of all Christians, Christ's blessed mother also shows herself a mother to them by her care and loving kindness. She never grows hard toward her children, as though they were not her own. The womb that once gave birth is not dried up; it continues to bring forth the fruit of her tender compassion. Christ, the blessed fruit of that womb, left his mother still fraught with inexhaustible love, a love that once came forth from her but remains always within her, inundating her with his gifts.

It can be seen that the children themselves recognize her as their mother. A natural instinct, inspired by faith, prompts them to have recourse to her in all dangers and difficulties, invoking her and taking refuge in her arms like little ones running to their mother. To this day we dwell in the shelter of the mother of the Most High, remaining under her protection as it were beneath the shadow of her wings. And in the days to come we shall share in her glory; we shall know the warmth of her loving embrace. Then there will be one joyful voice proclaiming the praise of our mother: Holy Mother of God, in you we all find our home!

(Sermon 1 on Mary's Assumption,
2-4: PL 185, 187-189)

Guerric of Igny (c.1070/1080-1157), about whose early life little is known, probably received his education at the cathedral school of Tournai, perhaps under the influence of Odo of Cambrai (1087-1092). He seems to have lived a retired life of prayer and study near the cathedral of Tournai. He paid a visit to Clairvaux to consult Saint Bernard, and is mentioned by him as a novice in a letter to Ogerius in 1125/1256. He became abbot of the Cistercian abbey of Igny, in the diocese of Rheims in 1138. A collection of 54 authentic sermons preached on Sundays and feast days have been edited. Guerric's spirituality was influenced by Origen.

Second Sunday After Christmas

Gospel: John 1:1-18 or 1-5.9-14

The Word of God became flesh and dwelt among us.

Commentary: Leo the Great

The infancy which the Son of God in his majesty did not disdain to assume developed with the passage of time into the maturity of manhood. After the triumph of the passion and the resurrection all the lowly acts he performed on our behalf are in the past. Nevertheless today's feast of Christmas renews for us the sacred beginning of the life of Jesus, son of the Virgin Mary, and we find that in celebrating our Savior's birth we also celebrate our own.

The birth of Christ is the origin of the Christian people, and the birthday of the head is also the birthday of the body. It is true that each of us is called in turn and that the children of the Church are separated from one another by being born at different times. Nevertheless, as the whole community of the faithful which comes into being in the baptismal font is crucified with Christ in his passion, raised up with him in his resurrection, and at his ascension placed at the right hand of the Father, so too it is born with him in his nativity. All over the world believers regenerated in Christ break with their former way of life that was marked by original sin, and by a second birth are transformed into new people. Henceforth they are reckoned to be of the stock, not of their earthly father, but of Christ, who became the Son of Man so that we could become children of God. Had he not so lowered himself as to come down to us, none of us could ever have gone to him by any merits of our own.

Therefore the greatness of the gift which he has bestowed on us demands an appreciation proportioned to its excellence; for blessed Paul the apostle truly teaches: *We have received not the spirit of the world, but the Spirit that comes from God to help us understand the gifts God has given us.* The only way that we can worthily honor him is by presenting to him what he himself has given us.

But what can we find in the treasury of the Lord's bounty more in keeping with the glory of this feast than that peace which was first announced by the angelic choir on the day of his birth? For peace makes us children of God; it nourishes love and is the mother of unity; it is the repose of the blessed and our home in eternity. The work of peace and its special blessing is to unite to God those whom it separates form the world.

Therefore, let those *who have been born not of blood, nor of the will of the flesh, nor of the will of a man, but of God,* offer to the Father their harmony as sons and daughters united in peace; and let all those whom he has adopted as his members meet in the firstborn of the new creation who came not to do his own will but the will of the one who sent him. The Father has not given the grace of being adopted as his heirs to people at variance with one another, possessing no common ground, but to those who are one in thought and love. Between the hearts and minds of those refashioned according to a single image there should be harmony.

The birthday of the Lord is the birthday of peace. As the Apostle says: *He is our peace, who has made us both one;* for whether we are Jews or Gentiles, *through him we have access in one Spirit to the Father.*

(*Sermon 6 on Christmas 2-3. 5: PL 54, 213-216*)

Leo the Great (c.400-461) was elected pope in 440. At a time of general disorder he did much to strengthen the influence of the Roman see. Although he was not a profound theologian, Leo's teaching is clear and forceful. His Tome was accepted as a statement of Christological orthodoxy at the Council of Chalcedon (451). One hundred and forty-three of his letters and ninety-six sermons have survived. The latter, which cover the whole of the liturgical year, have been published in a critical edition.

Epiphany

Gospel: Matthew 2:1-12

We have come from the East to worship the king.

Commentary: Basil the Great

The star came to rest above the place where the child was. At the sight of it the wise men were filled with great joy and that great joy should fill our hearts as well. It is the same as the joy the shepherds received from the glad tidings brought by the angels. Let us join the wise men in worship and the shepherds in giving glory to God. Let us dance with the angels and sing: *To us is born this day a savior who is Christ the Lord. The Lord is God and he has appeared to us,* not as God which would have terrified us in our weakness, but as a slave in order to free those living in slavery. Could anyone be so lacking in sensibility and so ungrateful as not to join us all in our gladness, exultation, and radiant joy? This feast belongs to the whole universe. It gives heavenly gifts to the earth, it sends archangels to Zechariah and to Mary, it assembles a choir of angels to sing, *Glory to God in the highest, and peace to his people on earth.*

Stars cross the sky, wise men journey from pagan lands, earth receives its savior in a cave. Let there be no one without a gift to offer, no one without gratitude as we celebrate the salvation of the world, the birthday of the human race. Now it is no longer, *Dust you are and to dust you shall return,* but "You are joined to heaven and into heaven you shall be taken up." It is no longer, *In sorrow you shall bring forth children,* but, "Blessed is she who has borne Emmanuel and blessed the breast that nursed him." *For a child is born to us, a son is given to us, and dominion is laid upon his shoulder.*

Come, join the company of those who merrily welcome the Lord from heaven. Think of shepherds receiving wisdom, of priests prophesying, of women who are glad of heart, as Mary was when told by the angel to rejoice and as Elizabeth was when John leapt in her womb. Anna announced the good news; Simeon took the child in his arms. They worshiped the mighty God in a tiny baby, not despising what they beheld but praising his divine majesty. Like light through clear glass the power of the Godhead shone through that human body for those whose inner eye was pure. Among such may we also be numbered, so that beholding his radiance with unveiled face we too may be transformed from glory to glory by the grace and loving kindness of our Lord Jesus Christ, to whom be honor and power for endless ages. Amen.

(Homily 2 on Christ's Origin, PG 31, 1472-1476)

Basil the Great (c.330-379), one of the three great Cappadocian Fathers, received an excellent education and began a career as a rhetorician before a spiritual awakening led him to receive baptism and become a monk. After visiting ascetics in Egypt, Palestine, Syria, and Mesopotamia, he decided that it was better for monks to live together in monasteries than alone as hermits, and he set about organizing Cappadocian monasticism. Basil's Rules influenced Saint Benedict. In 370 Basil succeeded Eusebius as bishop of Caesarea. His main concern was for the unity of the Church, and he strove to establish better relations between Rome and the East. His efforts bore fruit only after his death. Basil's writings include dogmatic, ascetic, and pedagogic treatises as well as letters and sermons.

Baptism of the Lord

Gospel: Matthew 3:13-17

When Jesus was baptized, the heavens were opened and the Spirit of God came upon him.

Commentary: Gregory the Wonderworker

I am the voice, the voice crying in the wilderness: Prepare the way for the Lord. So I cannot be silent, Lord, in your presence. *I need to be baptized by you, and do you come to me?* At my birth I took away my mother's barrenness, and while still an infant I healed my father's dumbness, for you gave me in childhood the gift of working miracles. But when you were born of the Virgin Mary, in the way you willed and in a manner known to you alone, you did not take away her virginity, but while preserving it intact you gave her in addition the name of "mother." Her virginity did not hinder your birth, nor did your birth destroy her viriginity. On the contrary, two opposites, motherhood and virginity, were easily united by you, because the laws of nature have their origin in you. I am a mere man, sharing in the grace of God, but you are both God and man because of your love for humankind.

I need to be baptized by you, and do you come to me? You existed from the beginning, you were with God and you were God. You are the radiance of the Father's glory, the perfect image of the perfect Father. *You are the true light enlightening every person who comes into the world.* You were in the world, yet you have come to where you were already. You have become flesh, but you have not been changed into flesh. You have lived among us, appearing to your servants in the likeness of a servant. You by your holy name have bridged heaven and earth, and do you come to me? You, so great, to such as I? King to herald, master to servant?

You were not ashamed to be born within the lowly limits of our human nature, but I cannot pass its bounds. I know the distance between the earth and the Creator, between the clay and the potter. I know how far I, a lamp lit by your grace, am outshone by you, the Sun of Righteousness. You are concealed by the pure cloud of your body, but I still recognize your sovereignty. I acknowledge my servile condition; I proclaim your greatness. I admit your absolute authority, and my own lowly estate. I am unworthy to undo the strap of your sandal; how then could I dare to touch your immaculate head? How could I stretch out my hand over you, who stretched out the heaven like a tent, and set the earth upon the waters? How could I enlighten the light? Surely it is not for me to pray over you, for you are the one who receives the prayers even of those who have no knowledge of you.

(Homily 4 on the Holy Manifestation: PG 10, 1181-1183)

Gregory the Wonderworker (c.213-270) was born of pagan parents, but became a Christian after attending a course of lectures given by Origen at Caesarea in Palestine. A few years later Phoedimus, bishop of Amasea, consecrated him the first bishop of Neocaesarea. So successful was his preaching that by the time he died he had converted from paganism practically the whole of Pontus. Gregory's panegyric on Origen provides valuable source material for the latter's life and method of teaching.

First Sunday of Lent

Gospel: Matthew 4:1-11

Jesus fasted for forty days and nights.

Commentary: Gregory Nazianzen

We must not expect baptism to free us from the temptations of our persecutor. The body that concealed him made even the Word of God a target for the enemy; his assumption of a visible form made even the invisible light an object of attack. Nevertheless, since we have at hand the means of overcoming our enemy, we must have no fear of the struggle. Flaunt in his face the water and the Spirit. In them will be extinguished all the flaming darts of the evil one.

Suppose the tempter makes us feel the pinch of poverty, as he did even to Christ, and taking advantage of our hunger, talks of turning stones into bread: we must not be taken in by him, but let him learn what he has still not grasped. Refute him with the word of life, with the word that is the bread sent down from heaven and that gives life to the world.

He may try to ensnare us through our vanity, as he tried to ensnare Christ when he set him on the pinnacle of the temple and said: "Prove your divinity: throw yourself down." Let us beware of succumbing to pride, for the tempter will by no means stop at one success. He is never satisfied and is always pursuing us. Often he beguiles us with something good and useful, but its end is always evil. That is simply his method of waging war.

We also know how well-versed the devil is in Scripture. When Christ answered the temptation to turn stones into bread with a rebuke from Scripture beginning: *It is written,* the devil countered with the same words, tempting Christ to throw himself down from the pinnacle of the temple. *For it is written,* he quoted, *he will give his angels charge of you, and on their hands they will bear you up.* O past master of all evil, why suppress the verse that follows? You did not finish the quotation, but I know full well what it means: that we shall tread on you as on an adder or a cobra; protected by the Trinity, we shall trample on you as on serpents or scorpions.

If the tempter tries to overthrow us through our greed, showing us at one glance all the kingdoms of the world—as if they belonged to him—and demanding that we fall down and worship him, we should despise him, for we know him to be a penniless impostor. Strong in our baptism, each of us can say: "I too am made in the image of God, but unlike you, I have not yet become an outcast from heaven through my pride. I have put on Christ; by my baptism I have become one with him. It is you that should fall prostrate before me." At these words he can only surrender and retire in shame; as he retreated before Christ, the light of the world, so will he depart from those illumined by that light. Such are the gifts conferred by baptism on those who understand its power; such the rich banquet it lays before those who hunger for the things of the Spirit.

(Homily 40, 10: PG 36, 370-371)

Gregory Nazianzen (329-389) was one of the three great Cappadocian Fathers. Desiring a retired, contemplative life, he became a monk, but in about 362 his father, the bishop of Nazianzus, ordained him priest against his will, and ten years later he was raised to the episcopate by his friend Saint Basil. In 379 Gregory was called to Constantinople, where his preaching helped to restore the Nicene faith and led to its final acceptance by the Council of Constantinople in 381. To the "Five Theological Orations" preached at Constantinople Gregory owes his title, "The Theologian."

Second Sunday of Lent

Gospel: Matthew 19:1-9

His face shone like the sun.

Commentary: Leo the Great

In the presence of chosen witnesses the Lord unveils his glory, investing with such splendor that bodily appearance which he shares with the rest of the human race that his face shines like the sun and his clothes become white as snow.

The primary purpose of this transfiguration was to remove the scandal of the cross from the hearts of Christ's disciples; the greatness of his hidden glory was revealed to them to prevent their faith being shaken by the self-abasement of the suffering he was voluntarily to undergo. In his foresight, however, he was also laying the foundations of the Church's hope, teaching the whole body of Christ the nature of the change it is to receive, and schooling his members to look forward to a share in the glory which had already shone forth in their head. The Lord had told them of this when he spoke of his coming in majesty: *Then shall the just shine like the sun in the kingdom of their Father.* The blessed apostle Paul bears witness to the same thing: *I consider that the sufferings of this present time are not worth comparing with the glory that is to be revealed in us.* And again: *You have died, and your life is hidden with Christ in God. When Christ who is your life appears, then you also will appear with him in glory.*

Still further instruction was to come from the transfiguration to fortify the apostles and perfect their understanding. Moses and Elijah, representing the law and the prophets, appeared in conversation with the Lord. Thus through the presence of these five men the saying was fulfilled: *On the evidence of two or three witnesses every word shall stand.* What could be more firmly established than that Word in whose proclamation the trumpets of Old and New Testaments sound in unison, and the writings of ancient witnesses are in perfect accord with the teaching of the gospel? The pages of both covenants agree with one another. He who had been promised beforehand by mysteriously veiled signs was now revealed clearly and distinctly in the radiance of his glory, since, as Saint John says, *The Law was given by Moses, but grace and truth have come through Jesus Christ.* In Christ what was promised by prophetic figures and what was signified by legal precepts are alike fulfilled, for by his presence he teaches the truth of the prophecies, and by grace he makes it possible for us to obey the commandments.

May we all therefore be confirmed in our faith through the preaching of the holy Gospel, and let no one be ashamed of the cross by which Christ has redeemed the world. None of us must be afraid to suffer for the sake of justice or doubt the fulfillment of the promises, for it is through toil that we come to rest and through death that we pass to life. If we continue in the acknowledgment and love of Christ who took upon himself all the weakness of our lowly nature, what he conquered we too shall conquer, and the promise he gave us we shall receive. So then, whether it is to encourage us to obey his commands or to endure hardships, let the Father's voice always be ringing in our ears and telling us: *This is my beloved Son in whom I am well pleased: listen to him.*

(Sermon 51, 3-4. 8: PL 54, 310-311. 313)

Leo the Great (c.400-461) was elected pope in 440. At a time of general disorder he did much to strengthen the influence of the Roman see. Although he was not a profound theologian, Leo's teaching is clear and forceful. His Tome was accepted as a statement of Christological orthodoxy at the Council of Chalcedon (451). One hundred and forty-three of his letters and ninety-six sermons have survived. The latter, which cover the whole of the liturgical year, have been published in a critical edition.

Third Sunday of Lent

Gospel: John 4:5-42 or 5-15.19b-26.39a.40-42

The water that I shall give will turn into a spring of eternal life.

Commentary: Augustine

W*earied by his journey, Jesus sat down beside a well. It was about the sixth hour.* Already divine mysteries begin. Not for nothing is Jesus wearied; not for nothing does the Power of God suffer fatigue. Not for nothing does he who refreshes the weary endure weariness. Not for nothing is he wearied, whose absence makes us weary, whose presence gives us strength.

Jesus is tired, tired out by his journey. He sits down. On the edge of a well he seats himself. It is midday, and he sits there exhausted. All these details have meaning. They are meant to signify something. They capture our attention, persuading us to knock and investigate further. We have Christ's own exhortation to do so, for he said: *Knock, and it will be opened to you.* May he, then, open up the meaning of this text to us as well as to you.

It was for your sake that Jesus was wearied by his journey. In Jesus we encounter divine power together with weakness. He is strong and weak at one and the same time: strong, because *in the beginning was the Word, and the Word was with God, and the Word was God, present with God from the beginning.* Would you know how strong the Son of God is? *All things were made through him, and apart from him nothing came into being.* The whole universe was made without effort. Could any greater power exist than the power of one who was able effortlessly to construct the entire universe?

And would you know him in his weakness? *The Word was made flesh, and lived among us.* The power of Christ created you; the weakness of Christ recreated you. Christ's power caused what did not exist to come into being; Christ's weakness saved existing things from destruction. In his might he fashioned us; in his weakness he came in search of us.

Jesus, then, is weak, tired out after his journey. Now that journey of his, undertaken for our sake, was his incarnation. How could he otherwise journey when he is present everywhere, and absent from nowhere? To what place or from what place could he travel? In only one way could he come to us, and that was by assuming our visible human flesh. Since then he condescended to come to us in that way, and to appear in the condition of a servant by taking to himself a human nature, that assumption of our nature was his journey.

The fatigue caused by his journey, therefore, was the weariness Jesus experienced in our human nature. In his human body he was weak, but you must not be weak. You must be strong in his weakness, for *there is more power in divine weakness than in human strength.*

(Homilies on the Gospel of John 15, 6-7:
CCL 36, 152-153)

Augustine (354-430) was born at Thagaste in Africa and received a Christian education, although he was not baptized until 387. In 391 he was ordained priest and in 395 he became coadjutor bishop to Valerius of Hippo, whom he succeeded in 396. Augustine's theology was formulated in the course of his struggle with three heresies: Manichaeism, Donatism, and Pelagianism. His writings are voluminous and his influence on subsequent theology immense. He molded the thought of the Middle Ages down to the thirteenth century. Yet he was above all a pastor and a great spiritual writer.

Fourth Sunday of Lent

Gospel: John 9:1-41 or 9:1.6-9.13-17.34-38

The blind man went off and washed himself and came away with his sight restored.

Commentary: Ambrose

You have heard that story in the gospel where we are told that the Lord Jesus, as he was passing by, caught sight of a man who had been blind from birth. Since the Lord did not overlook him, neither ought we to overlook this story of a man whom the Lord considered worthy of his attention. In particular we should notice the fact that he had been blind from birth. This is an important point.

There is, indeed, a kind of blindness, usually brought on by serious illness, which obscures one's vision, but which can be cured, given time; and there is another sort of blindness, caused by cataract, that can be remedied by a surgeon: he can remove the cause and so the blindness is dispelled. Draw your own conclusion: this man, who was actually born blind, was not cured by surgical skill, but by the power of God.

When nature is defective the Creator, who is the author of nature, has the power to restore it. This is why Jesus also said, *As long as I am in the world, I am the light of the world,* meaning: all who are blind are able to see, so long as I am the light they are looking for. Come, then, and receive the light, so that you may be able to see.

What is he trying to tell us, he who brought human beings back to life, who restored them to health by a word of command, who said to a corpse, *Come out!* and Lazarus came out from the tomb; who said to a paralytic, *Arise and pick up your stretcher,* and the sick man rose and picked up the very bed on which he used to be carried as a helpless cripple? Again, I ask you, what is he trying to convey to us by spitting on the ground, mixing his spittle with clay and putting it on the eyes of a blind man, saying: *Go and wash yourself in the pool of Siloam (a name that means "sent")?* What is the meaning of the Lord's action in this? Surely one of great significance, since the person whom Jesus touches receives more than just his sight.

In one instant we see both the power of his divinity and the strength of his holiness. As the divine light, he touched this man and enlightened him; as priest, by an action symbolizing baptism he wrought in him his work of redemption. The only reason for his mixing clay with the spittle and smearing it on the eyes of the blind man was to remind you that he who restored the man to health by anointing his eyes with clay is the very one who fashioned the first man out of clay, and that this clay that is our flesh can receive the light of eternal life through the sacrament of baptism.

You, too, should come to Siloam, that is, to him who was sent by the Father (as he says in the gospel, *My teaching is not my own, it comes from him who sent me).* Let Christ wash you and you will then see. Come and be baptized, it is time; come quickly, and you too will be able to say, *I went and washed;* you will be able to say, *I was blind, and now I can see,* and as the blind man said when his eyes began to receive the light, *The night is almost over and the day is at hand.*

(Letter 80, 1-5: PL 16, 1326-1327)

Ambrose (339-397) was born in Trier, the son of a praetorian prefect of Gaul. On the death of Auxentius, the Arian bishop of Milan, Ambrose, while still a catechumen, was elected to the see by acclamation. We know from Saint Augustine that as bishop he was accessible to everyone. Although Ambrose was influenced by the Greek Fathers, especially Origen, his preaching had the practical bent characteristic of Western theological writers.

Fifth Sunday of Lent

Gospel: John 11:1-45 or 11:3-7.17.20-27.33b-45

I am the resurrection and the life.

Commentary: Peter Chrysologus

On his return from the underworld, Lazarus comes forth from the tomb like death confronting its conqueror, an image of the resurrection to come. Before we can fathom the depths of meaning behind this miracle, we must consider the way in which our Lord raised Lazarus to life. This action appears to us as the greatest of all his signs; we see in it the supreme example of divine power, the most marvelous of all his wonderful works.

Our Lord had raised up the daughter of Jairus, the ruler of the synagogue; but although he restored life to the dead girl, he left the law of death still in force. He also raised the widow's only son. He halted the bier, forestalled the young man's burial, arrested the onset of physical decay; but the life he restored had not completely fallen into the power of death. The case of Lazarus was unique. His death and resurrection to life had nothing in common with the other two. Death had already exerted its full power over him, so that in him the sign of the resurrection shone out in all its fullness. I think it is possible to say that if Lazarus had remained only three days in the tomb it would have deprived our Lord's resurrection of its full significance, since Christ proved himself Lord by returning to life after three days, whereas Lazarus, as his servant, had to lie in the grave for four days before he was recalled. However, let us see if we can verify this suggestion by reading the gospel text further.

His sisters sent a message to Jesus saying, Lord, the friend whom you love is sick. By these words they appeal to his affection, they lay claim to his friendship, they call on his love, urging their familiar relationship with him to persuade him to relieve their distress. But for

Christ it was more important to conquer death than to cure disease. He showed his love for his friend not by healing him but by calling him back from the grave. Instead of a remedy for his illness, he offered him the glory of rising from the dead.

We are next told that *when Jesus heard that Lazarus was sick, he remained where he was for two days.* You see how he gives full scope to death. He grants free reign to the grave; he allows corruption to set in. He prohibits neither putrefaction nor stench from taking their normal course; he allows the realm of darkness to seize his friend, drag him down to the underworld, and take possession of him. He acts like this so that human hope may perish entirely and human despair reach its lowest depths. The deed he is about to accomplish may then clearly be seen to be the work of God, not of man.

He waited for Lazarus to die, staying in the same place until he could tell his disciples that he was dead; then he announced his intention of going to him. *Lazarus is dead,* he said, *and I am glad.* Was this a sign of his love for his friend? Not so. Christ was glad because their sorrow over the death of Lazarus was soon to be changed into joy at his restoration to life. *I am glad for your sake,* he said. Why for their sake? Because the death and raising of Lazarus were a perfect prefiguration of the death and resurrection of the Lord himself. What the Lord was soon to achieve in himself had already been achieved in his servant. This explains why he said to them: *I am glad for your sake not to have been there, because now you will believe.* It was necessary that Lazarus should die, so that the faith of the disciples might also rise with him from the dead.

(Sermon 63: PL 52, 375-377)

Peter Chrysologus (c.400-450), who was born at Imoly in Italy, became a bishop of Ravenna. He was highly esteemed by the Empress Galla Placidia, in whose presence he preached his first sermon as bishop. He was above all a pastor, and many of his sermons have been preserved.

Passion Sunday

Palm Sunday

Gospel: Matthew 21:1-11 (Blessing of Palms)

Blessed is he who comes in the name of the Lord.

Commentary: Gregory Palamas

Because of all he had done, the simple people believed in the Lord not only with a silent faith, but with a faith that proclaimed his divinity both by word and by deed. After raising Lazarus, who had been dead four days, the Lord found the young donkey his disciples had brought for him, as the evangelist Matthew relates. Seated on it he entered Jerusalem, in fulfillment of the prophecy of Zechariah: *Fear not, daughter of Zion; behold your king comes to you, the just one, the savior. He is gentle, and rides on a beast of burden, on the colt of a donkey.*

By these words the Prophet shows that Christ was the king he was foretelling, the only true king of Zion. He is saying: "Your king will not frighten those who look upon him; he is not an overbearing kind of person, or an evildoer. He does not come with a bodyguard, an armed escort, at the head of hosts of cavalry and foot soldiers. Nor does he live by extortion, demanding taxes and the payment of tribute and ignoble services, hurtful to those who perform them. No, he is recognized by his lowliness, poverty, and frugality, for he enters the city riding on a donkey, and with no crowd of attendants. Therefore, this king alone is just, and in justice he saves. He is also meek, meekness is his own special characteristic. In fact, the Lord's own words regarding himself were: *Learn from me, for I am meek and lowly in heart.*"

He who raised Lazarus from the dead enters Jerusalem today as king, seated on a donkey. Almost at once all the people, children and grown-ups, young and old alike, spread their garments on the road; and taking palm branches, symbols of victory, they went to meet him as the giver of life and conqueror of death. They worshipped him, and formed an escort. Within the temple precincts as well as without they sang with one voice, *Hosanna to the Son of David! Hosanna in the highest!* This *hosanna* is a hymn of praise addressed to God. It means, "Lord, save us." The other words, *in the highest*, show that God is praised not only on earth by human beings, but also on high by the angels of heaven.

(Homily XV: PG 151, 184-185)

Gregory Palamas (1296-1359) was born at Constantinople, and prepared by the piety of his parents for a monastic vocation. At the age of about 20 he became a monk of Mount Athos. In 1347 he was made bishop of Thessalonica. Gregory stressed the biblical teaching that the human body and soul form a single united whole. On this basis he defended the physical exercises used by the Hesychasts in prayer, although he saw these only as a means to an end for those who found them helpful. He followed Saint Basil the Great and Saint Gregory of Nyssa in teaching that although no created intelligence can ever comprehend God in his essence, he can be directly experienced through his uncreated "energies," through which he manifests himself to and is present in the world. God's substance and his energies are distinct from one another, but they are also inseparable. One of these energies is the uncreated divine light, which was seen by the apostles on Mount Tabor. At times this is an inward illumination; at other times it is outwardly manifested.

47

Gospel: Matthew 26:14-27.66 (Passion)

The account of the passion of our Lord Jesus Christ.

Commentary: Augustine

J*esus' hour had not yet come*—not the hour when he would be forced to die, but the hour when he would choose to be put to death. He knew the appointed hour for him to die; he had pondered all the prophecies concerning himself and was waiting until everything had taken place that the prophets said would occur before his passion began. When all was accomplished the passion would then follow, in the due ordering of events and not at the compulsion of fate.

Listen to these prophecies, and see if they are true. Among the other things that were foretold of Christ, it is written: *They mingled gall with my food, and in my thirst they gave me vinegar to drink.* How this came about we know from the gospel. First they gave Jesus gall; he took it, tasted it, and rejected it. Then, to fulfill the Scriptures as he hung on the cross, he said: *I am thirsty.* They took a sponge soaked in vinegar, tied it to a reed, and lifted it up to him where he hung. When he had taken it he said: *It is finished.* What did he mean by that? It is as though he said: "All the prophecies foretelling what would happen before my passion have been fulfilled. What then is left for me to do?" So, after saying *It is finished, he bowed his head and gave up his spirit.*

Did the thieves crucified beside him choose when to die? They were imprisoned in the flesh with no power over its limitations. But it was when he himself chose to do so that the Lord took flesh in a virgin's womb. He chose the moment of his coming among us and the duration of his life on earth. He also chose the hour when he would depart this earthly life. It was in his power to do all this; he was under no compulsion. So in waiting for the hour of his choice, not the hour decreed by fate, he made sure that everything that had to be fulfilled before he suffered was duly accomplished. How could Christ be subject to the decree of fate, when elsewhere he had said: *I have power to lay down my life, and I have power to take it up again. No one can take it from me; I lay it down of my own accord, and I will take it up again?* He showed that power when the Jewish authorities came in search of him. *Who are you looking for?* he asked them. *Jesus of Nazareth,* they answered, and he in turn replied: *I am he.* At these words they recoiled and fell to the ground.

Someone is sure to ask: If he had such power, why did he not demonstrate it when his enemies were taunting him and saying: *If he is the son of God, let him come down from the cross?* He was showing us how to endure; that was why he deferred the exercise of his power. If he were to come down because he was stung by their words, they would think he had succumbed to their mockery. He chose not to come down. He chose to stay where he was, refusing to die until the moment of his choice.

If Jesus had the power to rise from the tomb, could he have found it so very difficult to come down from the cross? We, then, for whom all these things were done, should understand that the power of our Lord Jesus Christ, which was then hidden, will be revealed at the Last Judgment. *Our God will come openly,* we are told. *He will no longer keep silence.* What does this mean? It means that previously when he was being judged he had been silent, in order to fulfill the prophecy: *He was led away like a sheep to be sacrificed; and like a lamb, dumb before the shearer, he did not open his mouth.*

Thus, unless he had been willing he would not have suffered, his blood would not have been shed; and if that blood had not been shed, the world would not have been redeemed. So let us pour out our thanks to him, both for the power of his divinity and for the compassion of his suffering humanity.

*(Homilies on the Gospel of John
37, 9-10: CCL 36, 336-338)*

Augustine (354-430) was born at Thagaste in Africa and received a Christian education, although he was not baptized until 387. In 391 he was ordained priest and in 395 he became coadjutor bishop to Valerius of Hippo, whom he succeeded in 396. Augustine's theology was formulated in the course of his struggle with three heresies: Manichaeism, Donatism, and Pelagianism. His writings are voluminous and his influence on subsequent theology immense. He molded the thought of the Middle Ages down to the thirteenth century. Yet he was above all a pastor and a great spiritual writer.

Evening Mass of the Lord's Supper

Gospel: John 13:1-15

To the end Jesus showed his love for them.

Commentary: Severian of Gabala

The whole visible world proclaims the goodness of God, but nothing proclaims it so clearly as his coming among us, by which he whose state was divine assumed the condition of a slave. This was not a lowering of his dignity, but rather a manifesting of his love for us. The awesome mystery which takes place today brings us to the consequence of his action. For what is it that takes place today? The Savior washes the feet of his disciples. Although he took upon himself everything pertaining to our condition as slaves, he took a slave's position in a way specially suited to our own arrangements when *he rose from the table.*

He who feeds everything beneath the heavens was reclining among the apostles, the master among slaves, the fountain of wisdom among the ignorant, the Word among those untrained in the use of words, the source of wisdom among the unlettered. He who nourishes all was reclining and eating with his disciples. He who sustains the whole world was himself receiving sustenance.

Moreover, he was not satisfied with the great favor he showed his servants by sharing a meal with them. Peter, Matthew, and Philip, men of the earth, reclined with him, while Michael, Gabriel, and the whole army of angels stood by. Oh, the wonder of it! The angels stood by in dread, while the disciples reclined with him with the utmost familiarity!

And even this marvel did not content him. *He rose from the table,* as Scripture says. He who is *clothed in light as in a robe* was clad in a cloak; he who wraps the heavens in clouds wrapped round himself a towel; he who pours the water into the rivers and pools tipped some water into a basin. And he before whom every knee bends in heaven and on earth and under the earth, knelt to wash the feet of his disciples.

The Lord of all creation washed his disciples' feet! This was not an affront to his dignity, but a demonstration of his boundless love for us. Yet however great his love was, Peter was well aware of his majesty. Always impetuous and quick to profess his faith, he was quick also to recognize the truth. The other disciples had let the Lord wash their feet, not with indifference, but with fear and trembling. They dared not oppose the Master. Out of reverence, however, Peter would not permit it. He said: *Lord, are you going to wash my feet? You shall never wash my feet!*

Peter was adamant. He had the right feelings, but not understanding the full meaning of the incarnation, he first refused in a spirit of faith, and afterward gratefully obeyed. This is how religious people ought to behave. They should not be obdurate in their decisions, but should surrender to the will of God. For although Peter reasoned in human fashion, he changed his mind out of love for God.

(Homily on the Washing of the Feet
in A. Wenger, Revue des Etudes Byzantines, 227-229)

Severian (c.400), bishop of Gabala in Syria, was a strong opponent of Saint John Chrysostom and took part in the intrigues that led to his condemnation by the Synod of Oak. According to Palladius he was also responsible for the transfer of the exiled Patriarch from Cucusus to Pityus. which resulted in his death. Severian is important as an exegete of the strict Antiochene school. He had some popularity as a preacher.

Good Friday

Gospel: John 19:17-30

The account of the passion of our Lord Jesus Christ.

Commentary: Cyril of Alexandria

They took Jesus in charge and carrying his own cross he went out of the city to what was called the Place of the Skull, or in Hebrew, Golgotha. There they crucified him.

They led away the author of life to die—to die for our sake. In a way beyond our understanding, the power of God brought from Christ's passion an end far different from that intended by his enemies. His sufferings served as a snare for death and rendered it powerless. The Lord's death proved to be our restoration to immortality and newness of life.

Condemned to death though innocent, he went forward bearing on his shoulders the cross upon which he was to suffer. He did this for our sake, taking on himself the punishment which the Law justly imposed upon sinners. *He was accursed for our sake according to the saying of Scripture: "A curse is on everyone who is hanged on a tree."* We who have all committed many sins were under that ancient curse for our refusal to obey the law of God. To set us free he who was without sin took that curse upon himself. Since he is God who is above all, his sufferings sufficed for all, his death in the flesh was the redemption of all.

And so Christ carried the cross, a cross that was rightfully not his but ours, who were under the condemnation of the Law. As he was numbered among the dead not on his own account but on ours, to destroy the power of death and to become for us the source of eternal life, so he accepted the cross we deserved. He passed the Law's sentence on himself *to seal the lips of lawlessness for ever,* as the psalm says, by being condemned sinless as he was for the sin of all.

Christ's example of courage in God's service will be of great profit to us, for only by putting the love of God before our earthly life and being prepared when occasion demands to fight zealously for the truth can we attain the supreme blessing of perfect union with God. Indeed, our Lord Jesus Christ has warned us that anyone who does not take up his cross and follow him is not worthy of him. And I think taking up the cross means simply renouncing the world for God's sake and, if this is required of us, putting the hope of future blessings before the life we now live in the body. Our Lord Jesus Christ was not ashamed to carry the cross we deserved, and he did so because he loved us.

Those united to Christ are also crucified with him by dying to their former way of life and entering upon a new life based on the teaching of the Gospel. Paul spoke for all when he said: *I have been crucified with Christ and the life I live now is not my life, but the life that Christ lives in me.*

(*Commentary on Saint John's Gospel*
12, 19: PG 74, 650-654)

Cyril of Alexandria (d.444) succeeded his uncle Theophilus as patriarch in 412. Until 428 the pen of this brilliant theologian was employed in exegesis and polemics against the Arians; after that date it was devoted almost entirely to refuting the Nestorian heresy. The teaching of Nestorius was condemned in 431 by the Council of Ephesus at which Cyril presided, and Mary's title, Mother of God, was solemnly recognized. The incarnation is central to Cyril's theology. Only if Christ is consubstantial with the Father and with us can he save us, for the meeting ground between God and ourselves is the flesh of Christ. Through our kinship with Christ, the Word made flesh, we become children of God, and share in the filial relation of the Son with the Father.

Easter Vigil

Gospel: John 20:1-9

The teaching of scripture is that Jesus must rise from the dead.

Commentary: John Chrysostom

How shall I recount for you these hidden realities or proclaim what surpasses every word and concept? How shall I lay open before you the mystery of the Lord's resurrection, the saving sign of his cross and of his three days' death? For each and every event that happened to our Savior is an outward sign of the mystery of our redemption.

Just as Christ was born from his mother's inviolate virginal womb, so too he rose again from the closed tomb. As he, the only-begotten Son of God, was made the firstborn of his mother, so, by his resurrection, he became the firstborn from the dead. His birth did not break the seal of his mother's virginal integrity; nor did his rising from the dead break the seals on the sepulchre. And so, just as I cannot fully express his birth in words, neither can I wholly encompass his going forth from the tomb.

Come, see the place where he lay. Come, see the place where the outward signs of your own resurrection are portrayed, where death lies entombed. Come, see the place where the unsown seed of mortality has brought forth a rich harvest of immortality.

Go and tell my brethren to go into Galilee, and there they will see me. Tell my disciples the mysteries which you yourselves have beheld. Thus did our Lord speak to the women. And still today, to those who believe, he is present, although unseen, in the baptismal font. As friends and brethren he embraces the newly baptized; with rejoicing and gladness he fills their hearts and souls. The Lord himself washes away their stains with streams of grace and anoints those who have been reborn with the precious ointment of the Spirit. The Lord becomes not only the one who feeds them, but also their very food; to his own servants he offers the daily largess of spiritual bread. To all the faithful he says, "Take and eat the bread from heaven; receive from my side the spring of water, ever flowing and never dried up. Let those who are hungry have their fill; let those who are thirsty drink the wine that brings true fulfillment and salvation."

O Christ our God, you alone are the good Lord and lover of all; to you, with the Father of all purity and the life-giving Spirit, belong the power and the glory, now and always and for endless ages. Amen.

(Homily on Holy Saturday 10-11, 12; PG 88, 1859-1866)

John Chrysostom (c.347-407) was born at Antioch and studied under Diodore of Tarsus, the leader of the Antiochene school of theology. After a period of great austerity as a hermit, he returned to Antioch where he was ordained deacon in 381 and priest in 386. From 386 to 397 it was his duty to preach in the principal church of the city, and his best homilies, which earned him the title "Chrysostomos" or "the golden-mouthed," were preached at this time. In 397 Chrysostom became patriarch of Constantinople, where his efforts to reform the court, clergy, and people led to his exile in 404 and finally to his death from the hardships imposed on him. Chrysostom stressed the divinity of Christ against the Arians and his full humanity against the Apollinarians, but he had no speculative bent. He was above all a pastor of souls, and was one of the most attractive personalities of the early Church.

Easter Sunday

Gospel: John 20:1-9

The teaching of scripture is that he must rise from the dead.

Commentary: Hesychius of Jerusalem

The festival we celebrate today, is one of victory—the victory of the son of God, king of the whole universe. On this day the devil is defeated by the crucified one; our race is filled with joy by the risen one. In honor of my resurrection in Christ this day cries out: "In my journey I beheld a new wonder—an open tomb, a man risen from the dead, bones exulting, souls rejoicing, men and women refashioned, the heavens opened, and powers crying out: *Lift up your gates, you princes; be lifted up, you everlasting doors, that the king of glory may come in.* On this day I saw the king of heaven, robed in light, ascend above the lightning and the rays of the sun, above the sun and the sources of water, above the dwelling place of the angelic powers and the city of eternal life."

Hidden first in a womb of flesh, he sanctified human birth by his own birth; hidden afterward in the womb of the earth, he gave life to the dead by his resurrection. Suffering, pain, and sighs have now fled away. For who has known the mind of God, or who has been his counselor if not the Word made flesh, who was nailed to the cross, who rose from the dead, and who was taken up into heaven?

This day brings a message of joy: it is the day of the Lord's resurrection when, with himself, he raised up the race of Adam. Born for the sake of human beings, he rose from the dead with them. On this day paradise is opened by the risen one, Adam is restored to life and Eve is consoled. On this day the divine call is heard, the kingdom is prepared, we are saved and Christ is adored. On this day, when he had trampled death under foot, made the tyrant a prisoner, and despoiled the underworld, Christ ascended into heaven as a king in victory, as a ruler in glory, as an invincible charioteer. He said to the Father: Here am I, O God, with the children you have given me and he heard the Father's reply: *Sit at my right hand until I make your enemies your footstool.* To him be glory, now and for ever, through endless ages, amen.

(Easter Homily: SC 187, 66-69)

Hesychius of Jerusalem (d.c. 451) was a monk who about 412 was highly esteemed as a priest and preacher in Jerusalem. He was a defender of orthodoxy and a gifted interpreter of scripture. His surviving homilies show that he followed the Alexandrian method of exegesis.

Second Sunday of Easter

Gospel: John 20:19-31

After eight days Jesus came in and stood among them.

Commentary: Cyril of Alexandria

By his miraculous entry through closed doors Christ proved to his disciples that by nature he was God and also that he was none other than their former companion. By showing them his side and the marks of the nails, he convinced them beyond a doubt that he had raised the temple of his body, the very body that had hung upon the cross. He had destroyed death's power over the flesh, for as God, he was life itself.

Because of the importance he attached to making his disciples believe in the resurrection of the body, and in order to prevent them from thinking that the body he now possessed was different from that in which he had suffered death upon the cross, he willed to appear to them as he had been before, even though the time had now come for his body to be clothed in a supernatural glory such as no words could possibly describe.

We have only to recall Christ's transfiguration on the mountain in the presence of his holy disciples, to realize that mortal eyes could not have endured the glory of his sacred body had he chosen to reveal it before ascending to the Father. Saint Matthew describes how Jesus went up the mountain with Peter, James, and John, and how he was transfigured before them. His face shone like lightning and his clothes became white as snow. But they were unable to endure the sight and fell prostrate on the ground.

And so, before allowing the glory that belonged to it by every right to transfigure the temple of his body, our Lord Jesus Christ in his wisdom appeared to his disciples in the form that they had known. He wished them to believe that he had risen from the dead in the very body that he had received from the blessed Virgin, and in which he had suffered crucifixion and death, as the Scriptures had foretold. Death's power was over the body alone, and it was from the body that it was banished. If it was not Christ's dead body that rose again, how was death conquered, how was the power of corruption destroyed? It could not have been destroyed by the death of a created spirit, of a soul, of an angel, or even of the Word of God himself. Since death held sway only over what was corruptible by nature, it was in this corruptible nature that the power of the resurrection had to show itself in order to end death's tyranny.

When Christ greeted his holy disciples with the words: *Peace be with you*, by peace he meant himself, for Christ's presence always brings tranquility of soul. This is the grace Saint Paul desired for believers when he wrote: *The peace of Christ, which passes all understanding, will guard your hearts and minds.* The peace of Christ, which passes all understanding, is in fact the Spirit of Christ, who fills those who share in him with every blessing.

(Commentary on Saint John's Gospel 12: PG 74, 704-705)

Cyril of Alexandria (d.444) succeeded his uncle Theophilus as patriarch in 412. Until 428 the pen of this brilliant theologian was employed in exegesis and polemics against the Arians; after that date it was devoted almost entirely to refuting the Nestorian heresy. The teaching of Nestorius was condemned in 431 by the Council of Ephesus at which Cyril presided, and Mary's title, Mother of God, was solemnly recognized. The incarnation is central to Cyril's theology. Only if Christ is consubstantial with the Father and with us can he save us, for the meeting ground between God and ourselves is the flesh of Christ. Through our kinship with Christ, the Word made flesh, we become children of God, and share in the filial relation of the Son with the Father.

Third Sunday of Easter

Gospel: Luke 24:13-35

They recognized Jesus at the breaking of the bread.

Commentary: Twelfth century author

Their eyes were opened, and they knew him when he broke the bread.
When bread is broken, it is in a way diminished, or "emptied." By
breaking understand the virtue of humility, by which Christ—even he
who is the bread of life— broke, diminished, and emptied himself. And
by emptying himself he gave us knowledge of himself.

The hidden Wisdom of the Father, and a treasure whole and
concealed—what use are they? Break your bread for the hungry, Lord,
the bread that is yourself, so that human eyes may be opened, and it
may not be regarded as a sin for us to long to be like you, knowing
good and evil. Let him who from the beginning wished to strive after
or grope for you in your undiminished state, know you through the
breaking of bread.

Break yourself that we may learn to break our own selves, for you
are not known through the breaking of bread. Balaam heard the words
of God and saw visions of the Almighty, but he fell with open eyes
because he did not know the Lord through the breaking of bread. It is
the same today: you see many studying the Scriptures, teaching in
cathedrals, preaching in churches, but their works do not agree with
their words. With words they claim to have a knowledge of God, but
with their deeds they deny it, because God cannot be known except
through the breaking of bread.

And in fact, the Lord became our bread and we are his bread. He
condescended to eat his bread with sweat on his brow, so that we might
eat with joy. If you want to know him, break yourself as he did, because
anyone who claims to abide in Christ ought to live as he lived. The
kingdom of God lies not in words, but in power.

Break yourself, then, by the labor of obedience, by the humiliation of repentance. Bear in your body the marks of Jesus Christ by accepting the condition of a servant, not of a superior. And when you have emptied yourself, you will know the Lord through the breaking of bread. True humility opens our eyes, "breaking" and diminishing the other virtues which might blind us with a spirit of pride, and teaching us that of ourselves we are nothing. And when we humble ourselves by self-contempt, so much the more do we grow in the knowledge of God.

(Sermon for Easter Monday: PL 184, 978-979)

Fourth Sunday of Easter

Gospel: John 10:1-10

I am the gate of the sheepfold.

Commentary: Clement of Alexandria

In our sickness we need a savior, in our wanderings a guide, in our blindness someone to show us the light, in our thirst the fountain of living water which quenches for ever the thirst of those who drink from it. We dead people need life, we sheep need a shepherd, we children need a teacher, the whole world needs Jesus!

If we would understand the profound wisdom of the most holy shepherd and teacher, the ruler of the universe and the Word of the Father, when using an allegory he calls himself the shepherd of the sheep, we can do so for he is also the teacher of little ones.

Speaking at some length through Ezekiel to the Jewish elders, he gives them a salutary example of true solicitude. I will bind up the injured, he says; I will heal the sick; I will bring back the strays and pasture them on my holy mountain. These are the promises of the Good Shepherd.

Pasture us children like sheep, Lord. Fill us with your own food, the food of righteousness. As our guide we pray you to lead us to your holy mountain, the Church on high, touching the heavens.

I will be their shepherd, he says, *and I will be close to them,* like their own clothing. He desires to save my flesh by clothing it in the robe of immortality and he has anointed my body. *They shall call on me,* he says, *and I will answer, "Here I am."* Lord, you have heard me more quickly than I ever hoped! *And if they pass over they shall not fall says the Lord,* meaning that we who are passing over into immortality shall not fall into corruption, for he will preserve us. He has said he would and to do so is his own wish. Such is our Teacher, both good and just. He said he had not come to be served but to serve,

62

and so the gospel shows him tired out, he who labored for our sake and promised *to give his life as ransom for many,* a thing which, as he said, only the Good Shepherd will do.

How bountiful the giver who for our sake gives his most precious possession, his own life! He is a real benefactor and friend, who desired to be our brother when he might have been our Lord, and who in his goodness even went so far as to die for us!

(The Teacher 9, 83, 3-85, a: SC 70, 258-261)

Clement of Alexandria (c.150-215) was born at Athens of pagan parents. Nothing is known of his early life nor of the reasons for his conversion. He was the pupil and the assistant of Pantaenus, the director of the catechetical school of Alexandria, whom he succeeded about the year 200. In 202 Clement left Alexandria because of the persecution of Septimus Severus, and resided in Cappadocia with his pupil, Alexander, later bishop of Jerusalem. Clement may be considered the founder of speculative theology. He strove to protect and deepen faith by the use of Greek philosophy. Central in his teaching is his doctrine of the Logos, who as divine reason is the teacher of the world and its lawgiver. Clement's chief work is the trilogy, "Exhortation to the Greeks," "The Teacher," and "Miscellanies."

Fifth Sunday of Easter

Gospel: John 14:1-12

I am the way, the truth, and the life.

Commentary: Ambrose

Let us march forward intrepidly to meet our Redeemer, Jesus, pursuing our onward course without swerving until we come to the assembly of the saints and are welcomed by the company of the just. It is to join our Christian forebears that we are journeying, to those who taught us our faith—that faith which comes to our aid and safeguards our heritage for us even when we have no good works to show. In the place we are making for the Lord will be everyone's light; the true light which enlightens every human person will shine upon all. In the house where we are going the Lord Jesus has prepared many dwelling-places for his servants, so that where he is we also may be, for this was his desire. Hear his own words about them: *In my Father's house are many dwelling-places,* and about his desire: *I will come again,* he says, *and take you to myself, so that where I am you also may be.*

"But he was speaking only to his disciples" you say, "and so it was to them alone that the many dwelling-places were promised." Do you really suppose it was only for the eleven disciples they were prepared? And what of the saying about people coming from all the corners of the earth to sit at table in the kingdom of heaven? Do we doubt that the divine will will be accomplished? But for Christ, to will is to do! Accordingly he has shown us both the way and the place: *You know where I am going,* he said, *and you know the way.* The place is where the Father is; the way is Christ, according to his own declaration: *I am the way, and the truth and the life; no one comes to the Father except through me.* Let us set out on this way, let us hold fast to truth, let us follow life. It is the way that leads us, the truth that strengthens us, the life that is restored to us through him.

To make sure that we really understand his will, Christ prays later on: *Father, it is my desire that those whom you have given me may be with me where I am, so that they may see my glory.* How graciously he asks for what he had already promised! The promise came first and then the request, not the other way around. Conscious of his authority and knowing the gift was at his own disposal, he made the promise; then, as if to show his filial submission, he asked his Father to grant it. He promised first to make us aware of his power; he asked afterwards to show us his loving deference to his Father.

Yes, Lord Jesus, we do follow you, but we can only come at your bidding. No one can make the ascent without you, for you are our way, our truth, our life, our strength, our confidence, our reward. Be the way that receives us, the truth that strengthens us, the life that invigorates us.

(Death as a Blessing 12, 52-55: CSEL 32, 747-750)

Ambrose (339-397) was born in Trier, the son of a praetorian prefect of Gaul. On the death of Auxentius, the Arian bishop of Milan, Ambrose, while still a catechumen, was elected to the see by acclamation. We know from Saint Augustine that as bishop he was accessible to everyone. Although Ambrose was influenced by the Greek Fathers, especially Origen, his preaching had the practical bent characteristic of Western theological writers.

Sixth Sunday of Easter

Gospel: John 14:15-21

I will ask the Father, and he will give you another Counselor.

Commentary: John Chrysostom

If you love me, said Christ, *keep my commandments.* I have commanded you to love one another and to treat one another as I have treated you. To love me is to obey these commands, to submit to me your beloved. *And I will ask the Father, and he will give you another Counselor.* This promise shows once again Christ's consideration. Because his disciples did not yet know who he was, it was likely that they would greatly miss his companionship, his teaching, his actual physical presence, and be completely disconsolate when he had gone. Therefore he said: *I will ask the Father, and he will give you another Counselor,* meaning another like himself.

They received the Spirit after Christ had purified them by his sacrifice. The Spirit did not come down on them while Christ was still with them, because this sacrifice had not yet been offered. But when sin had been blotted out and the disciples, sent out to face danger, were preparing themselves for the battle, they needed the Holy Spirit's coming to encourage them. If you ask why the Spirit did not come immediately after the resurrection, this was in order to increase their gratitude for receiving him by increasing their desire. They were troubled by nothing as long as Christ was with them, but when his departure had left them desolate and very much afraid, they would be most eager to receive the Spirit.

He will remain with you, Christ said, meaning his presence with you will not be ended by death. But since there was a danger that hearing of a Counselor might lead them to expect another incarnation and to think they would be able to see the Holy Spirit, he corrected this idea by saying: *The world cannot receive him because it does not*

66

see him. For he will not be with you in the same way as I am, but will dwell in your very souls, *He will be in you.*

Christ called him the Spirit of truth because the Spirit would help them to understand the types of the old law. By *He will be with you* he meant, *He will be with you as I am with you,* but he also hinted at the difference between them, namely, that the spirit would not suffer as he had done, nor would he ever depart.

The world cannot receive him because it does not see him. Does this imply that the Spirit is visible? By no means; Christ is speaking here of knowledge, for he adds: *or know him.* Sight being the sense by which we perceive things most distinctly, he habitually used this sense to signify knowledge. By *the world* he means here the wicked, thus giving his disciples the consolation of receiving a special gift. He said that the Spirit was another like himself, that he would not leave them, that he would come to them just as he himself had come, and that he would remain in them. Yet even this did not drive away their sadness, for they still wanted Christ himself and his companionship. So to satisfy them he said: *I will not leave you orphans; I will come back to you.* Do not be afraid, for when I promised to send you another counselor I did not mean that I was going to abandon you for ever, nor by saying that he would remain with you did I mean that I would not see you again. Of course I also will come to you; *I will not leave you orphans.*

(Homily 75, 1:PG 59, 403-405)

John Chrysostom (c.347-407) was born at Antioch and studied under Diodore of Tarsus, the leader of the Antiochene school of theology. After a period of great austerity as a hermit, he returned to Antioch where he was ordained deacon in 381 and priest in 386. From 386 to 397 it was his duty to preach in the principal church of the city, and his best homilies, which earned him the title "Chrysostomos" or "the golden-mouthed," were preached at this time. In 397 Chrysostom became patriarch of Constantinople, where his efforts to reform the court, clergy, and people led to his exile in 404 and finally to his death from the hardships imposed on him. Chrysostom stressed the divinity of Christ against the Arians and his full humanity against the Apollinarians, but he had no speculative bent. He was above all a pastor of souls, and was one of the most attractive personalities of the early Church.

Ascension

Gospel: Matthew 28:16-20

All authority in heaven and on earth has been given to me.

Commentary: Gregory of Nyssa

The gospel describes the Lord's life upon earth and his return to heaven. But the sublime prophet David, as though unencumbered by the weight of his body, rose above himself to mingle with the heavenly powers and record for us their words as they accompanied the Master when he came down from heaven. Ordering the angels on earth entrusted with the care of human life to raise the gates, they cried: *Lift up your gates, you princes; be lifted up you everlasting doors. Let the King of glory enter.*

But because wherever he is he who contains all things in himself makes himself like those who receive him, not only becoming a man among human beings, but also when among angels conforming his nature to theirs, the gatekeepers asked: *Who is this King of glory?*

He is the strong one, they were told, mighty in battle, the one who is to grapple with and overthrow the captor of the human race who has the power of death. When this last enemy has been destroyed, he will restore us to freedom and peace.

Now the mystery of Christ's death is fulfilled, victory is won, and the cross, the sign of triumph, is raised on high. He who gives us the noble gifts of life and a kingdom has ascended into heaven, *leading captivity captive.* Therefore the same command is repeated. Once more the gates of heaven must open for him. Our guardian angels, who have now become his escorts, order them to be flung wide so that he may enter and regain his former glory. But he is not recognized in the soiled garments of our life, in clothes reddened by the winepress of human sin. Again the escorting angels are asked: *Who is this King of glory?* The answer is no longer, *The strong one, mighty in battle* but,

The lord of hosts, he who has gained power over the whole universe, who has recapitulated all things in himself, who is above all things, who has restored all creation to its former state: *He is the King of glory.*

You see how much David has added to our joy in this feast and contributed to the gladness of the Church. Therefore as far as we can let us imitate the prophet by our love for God, by gentleness and by patience with those who hate us. Let the prophet's teaching help us to live in a way pleasing to God in Christ Jesus our Lord, to whom be glory for ever and ever. Amen.

(Sermon on the Ascension: Jaeger 9, 1, 323-327)

Gregory of Nyssa (c.330-395), the younger brother of Basil the Great, chose a secular career and married. Reluctantly, however, in 371, he received episcopal ordination and became bishop of Nyssa, an unimportant town in Basil's metropolitan district of Caesarea. Gregory was the greatest speculative theologian of the three Cappadocian Fathers, and the first after Origen to attemp a systematic presentation of the Christian faith. Gifted spiritually as well as intellectually, he has been called "the father of Christian mysticism." His spiritual interpretation of Scripture shows the influence of Origen.

Seventh Sunday of Easter

Gospel: John 17:1-11

Father, glorify your Son.

Commentary: Cyril of Alexandria

When the Savior declares that he has made known the name of God the Father, it is the same as saying that he has shown the whole world his glory. How did he do this? By making himself known through his wonderful works. The Father is glorified in the Son as in an image and type of his own form, for the beauty of the archetype is seen in its image. The only Son then has made himself known, and he is in his essence wisdom and life, the artificer and creator of the universe; he is immortal and incorruptible, pure, blameless, merciful, holy, good. His Father is known to be like him, since he could not be different in nature from his offspring. The Father's glory is seen, as in an image and type of his own form, in the glory of the Son.

The Son made known the name of God the Father to teach us and make us fully comprehend not that he is the only God, for inspired Scripture had proclaimed that even before the coming of the Son, but that besides being truly God he is also rightly called "Father." This is so because in himself and proceeding from himself he has a Son possessed of the same eternal nature as his own: it was not in time that he became the Father of the Creator of the ages!

To call God "Father" is more exact than to call him "God." The word "God" signifies his dignity, but the word "Father" points to the distinctive attribute of his Person. If we say "God" we declare him to be Lord of the universe; if we call him "Father" we show the way in which he is distinct as a Person, for we make known the fact that he has a Son. The Son himself gave God the name of Father, as being in some sense the more appropriate and truer appellation, when he said, not "I and God" but, *I and the Father are one,* and also, with reference to himself, *On him has God the Father set his seal.* And when he commanded his disciples to baptize all nations, he did not tell them to do this in the name of God, but expressly ordained that they were to do it in the name of the Father and of the Son and of the Holy Spirit.

*(Commentary on Saint John's Gospel 11, 7:
PG 74, 497-500)*

Cyril of Alexandria (d.444) succeeded his uncle Theophilus as patriarch in 412. Until 428 the pen of this brilliant theologian was employed in exegesis and polemics against the Arians; after that date it was devoted almost entirely to refuting the Nestorian heresy. The teaching of Nestorius was condemned in 431 by the Council of Ephesus at which Cyril presided, and Mary's title, Mother of God, was solemnly recognized. The incarnation is central to Cyril's theology. Only if Christ is consubstantial with the Father and with us can he save us, for the meeting ground between God and ourselves is the flesh of Christ. Through our kinship with Christ, the Word made flesh, we become children of God, and share in the filial relation of the Son with the Father.

Pentecost Sunday

Gospel: John 20:19-23

As the Father sent me, so I send you: Receive the Holy Spirit.

Commentary: Augustine

The happy day has dawned for us on which Holy Church makes her first radiant appearance to the eyes of faith and sets the hearts of believers on fire. It is the day on which we celebrate the sending of the Holy Spirit by our Lord Jesus Christ, after he had risen from the dead and ascended into glory. In the gospel it is written: *If anyone is thirsty, let him come to me and drink. Whoever believes in me, rivers of living water shall flow from his heart.* The Evangelist explains these words by adding: *Jesus said this about the Spirit which those who believed in him were to receive. For the Spirit had not yet been given because Jesus had not yet been glorified.* Now the glorification of Jesus took place when he rose from the dead and ascended into heaven, but all was not yet accomplished. The Holy Spirit still had to be given; the one who made the promise had to send him. This is precisely what occurred at Pentecost.

After being in the company of his disciples for the forty days following his resurrection, the Lord ascended into heaven, and on the fiftieth day—the day we are now celebrating—he sent the Holy Spirit. The account is given in Scripture: *Suddenly a sound came from heaven like the rush of a mighty wind, and there appeared to them tongues like fire which separated and came to rest on each one of them. And they began to speak in other tongues, as the Holy Spirit gave them power of utterance.* That wind cleansed the disciples' hearts, blowing away fleshly thoughts like so much chaff. The fire burnt up their unregenerate desires as if they were straw. The tongues in which they spoke as the Holy Spirit filled them were a foreshadowing of the Church's preaching of the Gospel in the tongues of all nations.

After the flood, in pride and defiance of the Lord, an impious generation erected a high tower and so brought about the division of the human race into many language groups, each with its own peculiar speech which was unintelligible to the rest of the world. At Pentecost, by contrast, the humble piety of believers brought all these diverse languages into the unity of the Church. What discord had scattered, love was to gather together. Like the limbs of a single body, the separated members of the human race would be restored to unity by being joined to Christ, their common head, and welded into the oneness of a holy body by the fire of love. Anyone therefore who rejects the gift of peace and withdraws from the fellowship of this unity cuts himself off from the gift of the Holy Spirit.

So then, my fellow members of Christ's body, you are the fruits of unity and the children of peace. Keep this day with joy, celebrate it in freedom of spirit, for in you is fulfilled what was foreshadowed in those days when the Holy Spirit came. At that time whoever received the Holy Spirit spoke in many languages, individual though he was. Now in the same way unity itself speaks through all nations in every tongue. If you yourselves are established in that unity you have the Holy Spirit among you, and nothing can separate you from the Church of Christ which speaks in the language of every nation of the world.

(Sermon 271: PL 38, 1245-1246)

Augustine (354-430) was born at Thagaste in Africa and received a Christian education, although he was not baptized until 387. In 391 he was ordained priest and in 395 he became coadjutor bishop to Valerius of Hippo, whom he succeeded in 396. Augustine's theology was formulated in the course of his struggle with three heresies: Manichaeism, Donatism, and Pelagianism. His writings are voluminous and his influence on subsequent theology immense. He molded the thought of the Middle Ages down to the thirteenth century. Yet he was above all a pastor and a great spiritual writer.

Trinity Sunday

Gospel: John 3:16-18

God sent his Son to save the world through him.

Commentary: Gregory Nazianzen

To speak of the Godhead is, I know, like crossing the ocean on a raft, or like flying to the stars with wings of narrow span. Even heavenly beings are unable to speak of God's decrees or of his government of the world. But enlighten my mind and loosen my tongue, Spirit of God, and I will sound aloud the trumpet of truth, so that all who are united to God may rejoice with their whole heart.

There is one eternal God, uncaused and uncircumscribed by any being existing before him or yet to be. He is infinite, and all time is in his hands. He is the mighty Father of one mighty and noble Son. In no way does the birth of this Son resemble human birth, for God is spirit. The Word of God is another divine Person, but not another Godhead. He is the living seal of the Father, the only son of the only God. He is equal to the Father, so that although the Father always remains wholly the Father, the Son is the creator and ruler of the world and is the Father's power and wisdom.

Let us praise the Son first of all, venerating the blood that expiated our sins. He lost nothing of his divinity when he saved me, when like a good physician he stooped to my festering wounds. He was a mortal man, but he was also God. He was of the race of David, but Adam's creator. He who has no body clothed himself with flesh. He had a mother, but she was a virgin. He who is without bounds bound himself with the cords of our humanity. He was victim and high priest—yet he was God. He offered up his blood and cleansed the whole world. He was lifted up on the cross, but it was sin that was nailed to it. He became as one among the dead, but he rose from the dead, raising to life also many who had died before him. On the one hand, there was the poverty of his humanity; on the other, the riches of his divinity. Do not let what is human in the Son permit you wrongfully to detract from what is divine. For the sake of the divine, hold in the greatest honor the humanity which the immortal Son took upon himself for love of you.

My soul, why do you hold back? Sing praise to the Holy Spirit as well, lest your words tear asunder what is not separated by nature. Let us tremble before the great Spirit who also is God, through whom we have come to know God, who transforms us into God. He is the omnipotent bestower of diverse gifts and the giver of life both in heaven and on earth. He is the divine strength, proceeding from the Father and subject to no power. He is not the Son, for there is only one Son, but he shares equally in the glory of the Godhead.

In the one God are three pulsations that move the world. Through them I became a new and different person when I came out of the font, where my death was buried, into the light—a man restored to life from the dead. If God cleansed me so completely, then I must worship him with my whole being.

(Poem 1-3: PG 37, 397-411)

Gregory Nazianzen (329-389) was one of the three great Cappadocian Fathers. Desiring a retired, contemplative life, he became a monk, but in about 362 his father, the bishop of Nazianzus, ordained him priest against his will, and ten years later he was raised to the episcopate by his friend Saint Basil. In 379 Gregory was called to Constantinople, where his preaching helped to restore the Nicene faith and led to its final acceptance by the Council of Constantinople in 381. To the "Five Theological Orations" preached at Constantinople Gregory owes his title, "The Theologian."

Corpus Christi

Gospel: John 6:51-59

My flesh is real food and my blood is real drink.

Commentary: Augustine

You see on God's altar bread and a cup. That is what the evidence of your eyes tells you, but your faith requires you to believe that the bread is the body of Christ, the cup the blood of Christ. In these few words we can say perhaps all that faith demands.

Faith, however, seeks understanding; so you may now say to me: "You have told us what we have to believe, but explain it so that we can understand it, because it is quite possible for someone to think along these lines: We know from whom our Lord Jesus Christ took his flesh—it was from the Virgin Mary. As a baby, he was suckled, he was fed, he developed, he came to young man's estate. He was slain on the cross, he was taken down from it, he was buried, he rose again on the third day. On the day of his own choosing, he ascended to heaven, taking his body with him; and it is from heaven that he will come to judge the living and the dead. But now that he is there, seated at the right hand of the Father, how can bread be his body? And the cup, or rather what is in the cup, how can that be his blood?"

These things, my friends, are called sacraments, because our eyes see in them one thing, our understanding another. Our eyes see the material form; our understanding, its spiritual effect. If, then, you want to know what the body of Christ is, you must listen to what the Apostle tells the faithful: *Now you are the body of Christ, and individually you are members of it.*

If that is so, it is the sacrament of yourselves that is placed on the Lord's altar, and it is the sacrament of yourselves that you receive. You reply "Amen" to what you are, and thereby agree that such you are. You hear the words "The body of Christ" and you reply "Amen."

Be, then, a member of Christ's body, so that your "Amen" may accord with the truth.

Yes, but why all this in bread? Here let us not advance any ideas of our own, but listen to what the Apostle says over and over again when speaking of this sacrament: *Because there is one loaf, we, though we are many, form one body.* Let your mind assimilate that and be glad, for there you will find unity, truth, piety, and love. He says, one loaf. And who is this one loaf? *We, though we are many, form one body.* Now bear in mind that bread is not made of a single grain, but of many. Be, then, what you see, and receive what you are.

So much for what the Apostle says about the bread. As for the cup, what we have to believe is quite clear, although the Apostle does not mention it expressly. Just as the unity of the faithful, which holy Scripture describes in the words: *They were of one mind and heart* in God, should be like the kneading together of many grains into one visible loaf, so with the wine. Think how wine is made. Many grapes hang in a cluster, but their juice flows together into an indivisible liquid.

It was thus that Christ our Lord signified us, and his will that we should belong to him, when he hallowed the sacrament of our peace and unity on his altar. Anyone, however, who receives this sacrament of unity and does not keep the bond of peace, does not receive it to his profit, but as a testimony against himself.

(Sermon 272: PL 38, 1246-1248)

Augustine (354-430) was born at Thagaste in Africa and received a Christian education, although he was not baptized until 387. In 391 he was ordained priest and in 395 he became coadjutor bishop to Valerius of Hippo, whom he succeeded in 396. Augustine's theology was formulated in the course of his struggle with three heresies: Manichaeism, Donatism, and Pelagianism. His writings are voluminous and his influence on subsequent theology immense. He molded the thought of the Middle Ages down to the thirteenth century. Yet he was above all a pastor and a great spiritual writer.

Sacred Heart

Gospel: Matthew 11:25-30

I am meek and humble of heart.

Commentary: Bruno of Segni

B*e imitators of God as his dearest children, and walk in love, just as Christ loved us and gave himself up for us as a sweet-smelling oblation and sacrifice.* Dearly beloved, in everything that he did and said our Lord Jesus Christ left us a pattern of humility, and instruction in virtuous living, for he wished to teach us not only by words, but also by example. Hence it is written: *Jesus began to do and to teach.* As regards humility the Lord himself said: *Learn from me, for I am meek and humble of heart.*

Although he was the almighty Lord, he chose to be poor for our sakes; he refused honors, freely submitted to sufferings, and even went so far as to pray for his persecutors. And he did all this in order that we might not disdain to follow him insofar as our frailty allows. If we fail to do so we are not true Christians, for anyone who says he loves Christ must tread the path he trod.

Because the Lord freely submitted to suffering and the cross, he delivered us by his very death from the power of the devil. Moreover, he prayed for sinners as he hung on the cross to give us an example. After all, if so much was willingly endured by the very Lord of the universe at the hands of slaves, by the just One at the hands of sinners, it behooves us to bear with the greatest patience wrongs done us by our own kith and kin.

And when we are in the midst of affliction, we too must pray most earnestly. Afflictions are of two kinds. It is an affliction when we suffer some temporal injury, and it is an affliction—a much greater one—when we give way to any kind of wrongdoing. Our prayer, however, must be such that it will not be turned into sin. And we must also give alms, and do so in the perfect way. The perfection of almsgiving consists in two things, namely, giving and forgiving. As the Lord says in the gospel: *Give and it will be given you; forgive and you will be forgiven.* These are the virtues through which we are to come to the kingdom of heaven, to which may our Lord Jesus Christ lead us, who lives and reigns for ever and ever.

(Sermon I for the Day before the Sabbath:
PL 165, 1007-1008)

Bruno of Segni (d.1123) was born near Asti in Piedmont, and studied at the university of Bologna before being made a canon of Siena. At the Council of Rome (1079) he defended the Catholic doctrine of the eucharist against Berengarius. In the following year Gregory VII, his personal friend, made him bishop of Segni, but he refused a cardinalate. Bruno was a zealous pastor, and shared in all the projects of Gregory VII for the reform of the Church. In his writings he attacked simony and lay investiture. He was the greatest Scripture commentator of his age. Longing for solitude, he received the monastic habit at Monte Cassino and in 1107 became abbot, but was later ordered by Pope Paschal II to return to his see.

Second Sunday
in Ordinary Time

Gospel: John 1:29-34

Behold the Lamb of God, who takes away the sins of the world.

Commentary: Cyril of Alexandria

When he saw Jesus coming toward him John said: *"Behold the Lamb of God, who takes away the sin of the world."* No longer does he say: *Prepare.* That would be out of place now that at last he who was prepared for is seen, is before our very eyes. The nature of the case now calls for a different type of homily. An explanation is needed of who is present, and why he has come down to us from heaven. So John says: *Behold the Lamb of God,* of whom the prophet Isaiah told us in the words: *He was led like a sheep to the slaughter, and like a lamb before his shearer he opened not his mouth.* In past ages he was typified by the law of Moses, but because the law was merely a figure and a foreshadowing its salvation was only partial; its mercy did not reach out to embrace the whole world. But now the true lamb, the victim without blemish obscurely prefigured in former times, is led to the slaughter for all to banish sin from the world, to overthrow the world's destroyer, to abolish death by dying for the entire human race, and to release us from the curse: *Dust you are and to dust you shall return.* He will become the second Adam who is not of earth but of heaven, and will be for us the source of every blessing. He will deliver us from the corruptibility foreign to our nature; he will secure eternal life for us, reconcile us with God, teach us to revere God and to live upright lives, and be our way to the kingdom of heaven.

One Lamb died for all to restore the whole flock on earth to God the Father; one died for all to make all subject to God; one died for all to gain all so that all *might live no longer for themselves, but for him who died and was raised to life for them.*

Because our many sins had made us subject to death and corruption, the Father gave his son as our redemption, one for all, since all were in him and he was greater than all. One died for all so that all of us might live in him. Death swallowed the Lamb who was sacrificed for all, and then disgorging him disgorged all of us in him and with him; for we were all in Christ who died and rose again for us.

Once sin had been destroyed how could death, which was caused by sin, fail to be wholly annihilated? With the root dead how could the branch survive? What power will death have over us now that sin has been blotted out? And so, rejoicing in the sacrifice of the Lamb let us cry out: *O death, where is your victory? O grave, where is your sting? All wickedness shall hold its tongue,* as the Psalmist sings somewhere. Henceforth it will be unable to denounce sinners for their weakness, for God is the one who acquits us. *Christ redeemed us from the curse of the law by becoming a curse for our sake,* so that we might escape the curse brought down on us by sin.

(Commentary on Saint John's Gospel 2: PG 73, 191-194)

Cyril of Alexandria (d.444) succeeded his uncle Theophilus as patriarch in 412. Until 428 the pen of this brilliant theologian was employed in exegesis and polemics against the Arians; after that date it was devoted almost entirely to refuting the Nestorian heresy. The teaching of Nestorius was condemned in 431 by the Council of Ephesus at which Cyril presided, and Mary's title, Mother of God, was solemnly recognized. The incarnation is central to Cyril's theology. Only if Christ is consubstantial with the Father and with us can he save us, for the meeting ground between God and ourselves is the flesh of Christ. Through our kinship with Christ, the Word made flesh, we become children of God, and share in the filial relation of the Son with the Father.

Third Sunday
in Ordinary Time

Gospel: Matthew 4:12-23 or 4:12-17

He went to Capernaum, that the prophecy of Isaiah might be fulfilled.

Commentary: John Justus Landsberg

The people who walked in darkness have seen a great light. Everyone knows that we were all born in darkness, and once lived in darkness. But now that the Sun of Righteousness has risen for us, let us see that we no longer remain in darkness.

Christ came to enlighten those who lived in darkness, overshadowed by death, and to guide their feet into the way of peace. Do you ask what darkness? Whatever is present in our intellect, in our will, or in our memory that is not God, or which has not its source in God; that is to say, whatever in us is not for God's sake, is a barrier between God and the soul—it is darkness.

In himself Christ brought us light which would enable us to see our sins, and hate our darkness. His freely chosen poverty, when there was no place for him in the inn, is for us a light by which we can now learn that the poor in spirit, to whom the kingdom of heaven belongs, are blessed.

The love with which Christ offered himself to instruct us, and to endure for us injuries, ostracism, persecution, lashes, and death upon a cross; the love finally which made him pray for those who crucified him—that love is for us a light by which we may learn to love our enemies.

The humility with which *he emptied himself, taking the nature of a slave,* and with which he scorned the glory of the world, and willed to be born, not in a palace but in a stable, and to die ignominiously on a gibbet—that humility is for us a light showing us what a detestable crime it is for clay, that is to say, for poor weak creatures, to be proud, to exalt themselves, or to refuse submission, when the infinite God was humbled, despised, and subject to human beings.

The meekness with which Christ endured hunger, thirst, cold, harsh words, lashes, and wounds, when he was *led like a sheep to the slaughter, and like a lamb before his shearer opened not his mouth*—that meekness is for us a light. By it we see how useless it is to be angry, how useless to threaten. By it we accept our own suffering, and do not serve Christ merely from routine. By it we learn how much is required of us, and that when suffering comes our way we should bewail our sins in silent submission, since he endured affliction with such patience and long-suffering, not for his own sins, but for ours.

Reflect then, beloved, on all the virtues which Christ taught us by his example, which he recommends by his counsel, and which he enables us to imitate by the assistance of his grace.

(Sermon 5, volume 3, 315-317)

Landsberg, John Justus (1489/90-1539), so called from the place of his birth in Bavaria, received the degree of Bachelor of Arts in Cologne, and then entered Saint Barbara's, the celebrated charterhouse there. He made his profession in 1509, and in due course was ordained a priest. From 1530 to 1534/35 he was prior of the charterhouse of Vogelsang, and at the same time preacher at the court of John III, duke of Juliers, Cleeves, and Berg, an unusual function for a Carthusian. He was one of the best spiritual writers of his day, the chief characteristic of his spirituality being the contemplation of Christ, the man-God, in his life, and in his passion and death. Landsberg was the editor of the works of Saint Gertrude, the great apostle in the Middle Ages of devotion to the Heart of Jesus, and he himself was one of the earliest promoters of this devotion.

Fourth Sunday in Ordinary Time

Gospel: Matthew 5:1-12

Blessed are the poor in spirit.

Commentary: Symeon the New Theologian

When holy Scripture is being read we should look at ourselves as though in a mirror and consider our state of soul. Let me explain what I mean. We hear the Lord saying: *Blessed are the poor in spirit, for theirs is the kingdom of heaven.* This must make us always examine and test ourselves whenever we suffer humiliation, whenever we are insulted, dishonored, and treated with contempt, to see whether or not we possess the virtue of humility. A person who has it bears everything without feeling hurt or taking offense. His heart is not wounded by anything that happens to him. If he is slightly wounded he is not completely upset; on the contrary, because of that heart wound, simply for having been slightly pained instead of accepting what happened with joy, he is distressed and thinks himself despicable, he grieves and weeps. Withdrawing into the inner chamber of his soul or his cell, he falls down before God and confesses to him as though he had completely forfeited eternal life.

Then again we hear: *Blessed are those who mourn.* Notice that the Lord does not say those who have mourned, but those who continually mourn. Concerning this too, then, we must examine ourselves to see whether we mourn every day, for if we have been made humble by repentance, obviously we shall not pass a single day or night without tears, without mourning, and without compunction.

And again: *Blessed are the gentle.* Can anyone who mourns every day continue to live in a state of anger and not become gentle? Just as water extinguishes a blazing fire, so mourning and tears extinguish anger in the soul so completely that a person who has long been given over to it sees his irascible disposition transformed into perfect serenity.

Again we hear: *Blessed are the merciful.* Who, then, are the merciful? Those who give away their possessions or who feed the poor? No. Then who are they? Those who have become poor for the sake of him who became poor for our sake, those who have nothing to give, but who in a spiritual way are always mindful of the poor, the widows, the orphans, and the sick. Seeing them frequently, they have compassion on them and shed burning tears over them. Such was Job, who said: *I wept over every infirmity.* When they have anything they cheerfully give alms to them, as well as ungrudgingly reminding all of how they can save their souls, thus obeying the one who said: *What I learned with pure intention I pass on without grudging.* These are the ones the Lord calls blessed, the ones who are truly merciful, for such mercy is like a step by which they ascend to attain perfect purity of heart.

In virtue of this God then proclaims the pure of heart blessed, saying: *Blessed are the pure of heart, for they shall see God.* The purified soul sees God in everything and is reconciled to him. Peace is established between God our creator and the soul, his erstwhile enemy, and it is then called blessed by God for being a peacemaker: *Blessed are the peacemakers,* he says, *for they shall be called children of God.*

(*Catechesis 31: SC 113, 226-230*)

Symeon the New Theologian (949-1022) was born in Galata in Paphlagonia, and educated in Constantinople, where in 977 he entered the famous monastery of Studies. Soon afterward he transferred to the nearby monastery of Saint Mamas, was ordained priest in 980, and about three years later became abbot. During his twenty-five years of office he instilled a new fervor into his community, but opposition to his teaching forced him to resign in 1005 and in 1009 he was exiled to Palonkiton on the other side of the Bosphorus. He turned the ruined oratory of Saint Marina into another monastery, and although he was soon pardoned, chose to remain there until his death rather than compromise his teaching.

Fifth Sunday
in Ordinary Time

Gospel: Matthew 5:13-16

Let your light shine before all.

Commentary: John Chrysostom

We who have once for all clothed ourselves in Christ, and been made worthy to have him dwelling within us, may show everyone, if we choose, simply by the strict discipline of our life and without saying a word, the power of him who dwells in us. Therefore Christ said: *Let your light so shine before all, that people may see your good works and praise your Father in heaven.* This is a light that reaches not only the bodily senses, but illuminates also the beholder's mind and soul. It disperses the darkness of evil, and invites those who encounter it to let their own light shine forth, and to follow the example of virtue.

Let your light shine before all, Christ said; and he used the words *before all* advisedly. He meant, "Let your light be so bright that it illuminates not only yourself, but shines also before those needing its help." As the light our senses perceive puts darkness to flight, and enables those travelling along a road perceptible to the senses to follow a straight course, so also the spiritual light which shines from blameless conduct illuminates those who cannot see clearly how to live a virtuous life, because their spiritual eyesight has been blurred by the darkness of error. It purifies their inward vision, leads them to live upright lives, and makes them walk henceforward in the path of virtue.

That people may see your good works and praise your Father in heaven. Christ means: Let your virtue, the perfection of your life, and the performance of good works inspire those who see you to praise the common Master of us all. And so I beg each of you to strive to live so perfectly that the Lord may be praised by all who see you. By the perfection of your lives attract to yourselves the grace of the Spirit, so that the Lord of all creation may be glorified, and so that we may all be found worthy of the kingdom of heaven by the grace, mercy, and goodness of God's only-begotten Son our Lord Jesus Christ, to whom with the Father and the Holy Spirit be glory, might, and honor now and for ever and for endless ages. Amen.

(Eighth Baptismal Catecheses 4, 18-26. 33:
SC 50, 192-193. 196. 199)

John Chrysostom (c.347-407) was born at Antioch and studied under Diodore of Tarsus, the leader of the Antiochene school of theology. After a period of great austerity as a hermit, he returned to Antioch where he was ordained deacon in 381 and priest in 386. From 386 to 397 it was his duty to preach in the principal church of the city, and his best homilies, which earned him the title "Chrysostomos" or "the golden-mouthed," were preached at this time. In 397 Chrysostom became patriarch of Constantinople, where his efforts to reform the court, clergy, and people led to his exile in 404 and finally to his death from the hardships imposed on him. Chrysostom stressed the divinity of Christ against the Arians and his full humanity against the Apollinarians, but he had no speculative bent. He was above all a pastor of souls, and was one of the most attractive personalities of the early Church.

Sixth Sunday
in Ordinary Time

Gospel: Matthew 5:17-37

Such was said to your ancestors, but I am speaking to you.

Commentary: John Chrysostom

Christ gave his life for you, and do you hold a grudge against your fellow servant? How then can you approach the table of peace? Your Master did not refuse to undergo every kind of suffering for you, and will you not even forgo your anger? Why is this, when love is the root, the wellspring and the mother of every blessing?

He has offered me an outrageous insult, you say. He has wronged me times without number, he has endangered my life. Well, what is that? He has not yet crucified you as the Jewish elders crucified the Lord. If you refuse to forgive your neighbor's offense your heavenly Father will not forgive your sins either. What does your conscience say when you repeat the words: *Our Father who art in heaven, hallowed be thy name,* and the rest? Christ went so far as to offer his blood for the salvation of those who shed it. What could you do that would equal that? If you refuse to forgive your enemy you harm not him but yourself. You have indeed harmed him frequently in this present life, but you have earned for yourself eternal punishment on the day of judgment. There is no one God detests and repudiates more than the person who bears a grudge, whose heart is filled with anger, whose soul is seething with rage.

Listen to the Lord's words: *If you are bringing your gift to the altar, and there remember that your brother or sister has something against you, leave your gift there before the altar and first go and be reconciled. Then come and offer your gift.* What do you mean? Am I really to leave my gift, my offering there? Yes, he says, because this sacrifice is offered in order that you may live in peace with your neighbor. If then the attainment of peace with your neighbor is the object of the sacrifice and you fail to make peace, even if you share in the sacrifice your lack of peace will make this sharing fruitless. Before all else therefore make peace, for the sake of which the sacrifice is offered. Then you will really benefit from it.

The reason the Son of God came into the world was to reconcile the human race with the Father. As Paul says: *Now he has reconciled all things to himself, destroying enmity in himself by the cross.* Consequently, as well as coming himself to make peace he also calls us blessed if we do the same, and shares his title with us. *Blessed are the peacemakers, he says, for they shall be called children of God.*

So as far as a human being can, you must do what Christ the Son of God did, and become a promoter of peace both for yourself and for your neighbor. Christ calls the peacemaker a child of God. The only good deed he mentions as essential at the time of sacrifice is reconciliation with one's brother or sister. This shows that of all the virtues the most important is love.

(Homily on the Treachery of Judas: Bareille, t. 3, 655-656)

John Chrysostom (c.347-407) was born at Antioch and studied under Diodore of Tarsus, the leader of the Antiochene school of theology. After a period of great austerity as a hermit, he returned to Antioch where he was ordained deacon in 381 and priest in 386. From 386 to 397 it was his duty to preach in the principal church of the city, and his best homilies, which earned him the title "Chrysostomos" or "the golden-mouthed," were preached at this time. In 397 Chrysostom became patriarch of Constantinople, where his efforts to reform the court, clergy, and people led to his exile in 404 and finally to his death from the hardships imposed on him. Chrysostom stressed the divinity of Christ against the Arians and his full humanity against the Apollinarians, but he had no speculative bent. He was above all a pastor of souls, and was one of the most attractive personalities of the early Church.

Seventh Sunday
in Ordinary Time

Gospel: Matthew 5:38-48

Love your enemies.

Commentary: Walter Hilton

When love acts in the soul it does so wisely and gently, for it has great power to kill anger and envy, and all the passions of wrath and melancholy, and it brings into the soul the virtues of patience, gentleness, peaceableness, and friendliness to one's neighbor. People guided only by their own reason find it very hard to be patient, peaceful, sweet-tempered and charitable to their neighbors when they treat them badly and wrong them. But true lovers of Jesus have no great difficulty in enduring all this, because love fights for them and kills such movements of wrath and melancholy with amazing ease. Through the spiritual sight of Jesus it makes the souls of such people so much at ease and so peaceful, so ready to endure and so conformed to God, that if they are despised and disregarded by others, or suffer injustice or injury, shame or ill-treatment, they pay no attention. They are not greatly disturbed by these things and will not allow themselves to be, for then they would lose the comfort they feel in their souls, and that they are unwilling to do. They can more easily forget all the wrong that is done them than others can forgive it even when asked for forgiveness. They would rather forget than forgive, for that seems easier to them.

And it is love that does all this, for love opens the eye of the soul to the sight of Jesus, and confirms it in the pleasure and contentment of the love that comes from that sight. It comforts the soul so much that it is quite indifferent to what others do against it. The greatest harm that could befall such people would be to lose the spiritual sight of Jesus, and they would therefore suffer all other injuries than that one alone.

When true lovers of Jesus suffer harm from their neighbors, they are so strengthened by the grace of the Holy Spirit and are made so truly humble, so patient, and so peaceable, that they retain their humility no matter what harm or injury is inflicted on them. They do not despise their neighbors or judge them, but they pray for them in their hearts, and feel more pity and compassion for them than for others who never harmed them, and in fact they love them better, and more fervently desire their salvation, because they see that they will have so much spiritual profit from their neighbors' deeds, though this was never their intention. But this love and this humility, which are beyond human nature, come only from the Holy Spirit to those whom he makes true lovers of Jesus.

(The Scale of Perfection II, 3, chapter 8—modernized)

Hilton, Walter (+1396), outstanding English mystic, seems to have studied theology and canon law, and after that to have lived for a time as a hermit. It is certain that he became an Augustinian canon at Thurgarton Priory in Nottinghamshire, England, where he eventually died. The *Scale of Perfection* is the best known of his writings, which also included works in Latin. The *Goad of Love* is an expanded translation of meditations by James of Milan.

Eighth Sunday in Ordinary Time

Gospel: Matthew 6:24-34

Do not worry about tomorrow.

Commentary: Attributed to Macarius of Egypt

Wishing to lead his disciples to perfect faith, the Lord said in the gospel: *Whoever is unbelieving in a small matter will be unbelieving also when it comes to something important; and whoever believes in a small matter will believe also when it comes to something important.* What are the small matters, and what the important ones?

The small matters are things offered by this world, which the Lord has promised to provide for those who believe in him—things such as food, clothing, and whatever else is necessary for the body's well-being, health, and the like. About these he commanded us not to have the slightest anxiety but confidently to trust him, for he will supply all the needs of those who make him their refuge. On the other hand, the important matters are the gifts pertaining to the eternal and incorruptible world, which he has promised to provide for those who believe in him, and who are ceaselessly concerned about these things and ask him for them as he commanded.

The Lord said: *Seek first the kingdom of God and his righteousness, and all these things will be yours as well.* Thus each person is to be tested by these trivial and transitory things to see whether he or she believes that God will supply them. We are to have no anxiety about such things, but are to be concerned solely with the eternal blessings to come. It will then be obvious that one believes in the incorruptible things and really does seek the eternal blessings, if one preserves a strong faith concerning the things we have spoken of.

All who submit to the word of truth should test and examine themselves, or else be tested and examined by spiritual counselors, as to the way they live out their belief and surrender themselves to God. Are they really living by God's word, or only by an imaginary belief based on a false notion of righteousness and faith?

It is regarding his faith in small matters, that is to say, in temporal matters, that each person is examined and tested. Hear how this is done. Do you say you believe that you have been deemed worthy of the kingdom of heaven, that you have been born from above as a child of God, that you are a co-heir with Christ, and that you will reign with him for ever, rejoicing like God in light brilliant beyond description throughout the untold ages of eternity? No doubt you will answer, "Yes, that is the very reason why I left the world and gave myself to the Lord."

Examine yourself, then, to see whether worldly cares may still have a hold on you; whether you are very preoccupied with feeding and clothing your body, and with your other pursuits and your recreation, as though your own power kept you alive, and you were obliged to make provision for yourself, when you have been commanded to have no anxiety whatever concerning yourself. If you believe that you will receive everlasting, eternal, abiding, and bounteous blessings, how much more should you not believe that God will provide you with these transitory, earthly benefits, which he has given even to impious people and to beasts and birds?

You who have become a stranger to the world ought to possess a faith, an outlook, and a manner of life which has about it something unusual, something different from that of all worldly people. Glory be to the Father and to the Son and to the Holy Spirit.

(Homily 48, 1-6: PG 34, 807-811)

Macarius, Pseudo (4th-5th century), formerly confused with Macarius of Egypt, probably came to the south of Asia Minor from Mesopotamia. Abbot of a community of cenobites, he must have been a monk of great spiritual stature and authority, for his influence on later monastic spirituality was profound. Accusations of Messalianism made him a highly controversial figure, but in many points his teaching is in fact anti-Messalian. He stresses the importance of continual prayer as did the Messalians, but not at the expense of work and service to others. The best known of his works are the *Fifty Spiritual Homilies,* but the complete corpus of his writings is now being edited.

Ninth Sunday
in Ordinary Time

Gospel: Matthew 7:21-27

A wise person builds his house on rock, not on sand.

Commentary: Philoxenus of Mabbug

Whoever listens to what I say and acts on it is like a wise man who dug deep down and built on rock; the rain fell, the floods came and the winds blew and beat upon his house, but it did not fall because it was built on rock.

This saying of our Master obliges us to be diligent not only in hearing God's word, but also in obeying it. We do well to Glisten to the law, because it moves us to good works; it is a good thing to read and meditate on Scripture, because our inmost thoughts are thus purified from all evil; but to be assiduous in reading, listening to and meditating on the law of God without doing what it says is a wickedness that the spirit of God has already condemned, forbidding those guilty of it even to pick up the holy book in their unclean hands. *God said to the sinner: Do not touch the book of my commandments, because you have taken my covenant on your lips, but have hated correction and cast my words behind you.*

Assiduous readers who do no good works are accused by their very reading, and merit a more severe condemnation because each day they scorn and despise what they have heard that day. They are like dead people, corpses without souls. The dead will not hear thousands of trumpets and horns sounding in their ears; in the same way souls dead in sin, minds that have forgotten God, do not hear the sound and cry of divine words; the spiritual trumpet leaves them unmoved. They sleep the sleep of death and find it pleasant.

God's disciples need to have firmly anchored in their souls the remembrance of their Master, Jesus Christ, and to think of him day and night. They must learn where to begin, and how and where to construct the rooms in their buildings, and how to bring those buildings to completion. Otherwise all the passers-by will mock them, as our Lord said about the man who set out to build a tower and could not finish it.

The foundation is already laid, as Saint Paul said: it is Jesus Christ our God. *If anyone builds on this foundation with gold or silver or precious stones, or with wood or straw or stubble, his work will be brought to light, because fire will reveal it and test the quality of each one's work.*

Good habits and righteousness in all their beauty are what Paul compared to gold, silver, and precious stones. Faith is like gold; temperance, fasting, abstinence, and the other good works are like silver; while the precious stones are peace, hope, pure and holy thoughts, and spiritual understanding that contemplates God and the grandeur of his being, and keeps silence, trembling before the inexplicable, uncommunicable mysteries of the Godhead.

(Homily 1: SC 44, 27-31)

Philoxenus (c.440-523), anti-Chalcedonian bishop of Mabbug (Hieropolis), was an outstanding theologian and master of the spiritual life, who achieved a remarkable synthesis between the Syriac and Greek traditions. He was exiled to Thrasia several years before his death. His extensive writings include thirteen orations on the Christian life, five treatises on the Trinity and Incarnation, and several letters. His name is preserved in "Philoxeniana," a Syriac translation of the Bible.

Tenth Sunday
in Ordinary Time

Gospel: Matthew 9:9-13

I did not come to call the righteous, but sinners to repentance.

Commentary: Augustine

Some people's strength is based on confidence in their own right-eousness. It was this kind of strength that prevented the Jewish leaders from entering the eye of the needle. They took their righteous-ness for granted and seemed in their own eyes to be healthy. Therefore they refused the remedy and slew the physician. They were strong, not weak. They were not the ones he came to call who said: *The healthy have no need of a physician; it is the sick who need him. I did not come to call the righteous but sinners to repentance.* Those were strong people who taunted Christ's disciples because their master entered the homes of the sick and ate with them. *Why,* they asked, *does your master eat with tax collectors and sinners?* O you strong ones who do not need the doctor! Yours is not the strength of health but of madness! God grant that we may never imitate that kind of strength. We should dread the possibility of anyone wanting to imitate it.

The teacher of humility, who shared our weakness and gave us a share in his own divinity, came to earth in order to teach us the way, even to be the Way himself. It was his humility, above all else, that he impressed upon us. He willingly submitted to baptism at the hands of one of his servants, so that we might learn to confess our own sins and to become weak in order to be truly strong, repeating with the Apostle: *When I am weak, then I am strong.*

But as for the people who wished to be strong, that is, those who wanted to be righteous by their own power, they tripped over the stumbling block. In their eyes, the Lamb was a goat, and because, seeing him as a goat, they killed him, they did not deserve to be redeemed by the Lamb. In their strength they attacked Christ, priding themselves on their own righteousness. Listen to these strong ones talking. They had sent some people from Jerusalem to arrest Christ but they did not dare to do so. *Why did you not seize him?* they demanded. *No one ever spoke like this man,* they replied. To which the strong ones retorted: *You do not see any of the Pharisees believing in him, do you, or any of the Scribes? It is only the people who are ignorant of the law that believe in him.*

Thus they put themselves on a higher level than the weak crowd that ran to the doctor. Why did they exalt themselves? Because they were strong. What is worse, by their strength they drew the whole crowd to themselves and killed the physician who had power to heal them all. But the murdered physician, by his very death, compounded a medicine for the sick out of his own blood.

(Exposition of the Psalms 58, I, 7: CCL 39, 733-734)

Augustine (354-430) was born at Thagaste in Africa and received a Christian education, although he was not baptized until 387. In 391 he was ordained priest and in 395 he became coadjutor bishop to Valerius of Hippo, whom he succeeded in 396. Augustine's theology was formulated in the course of his struggle with three heresies: Manichaeism, Donatism, and Pelagianism. His writings are voluminous and his influence on subsequent theology immense. He molded the thought of the Middle Ages down to the thirteenth century. Yet he was above all a pastor and a great spiritual writer.

Eleventh Sunday
in Ordinary Time

Gospel: Matthew 9:36–10:8

He summoned his twelve disciples, and sent them out.

Commentary: John Chrysostom

All farm work is undertaken with a view to the harvest that will come at the end. How then could Jesus apply the word "harvest" to work that was only beginning? Idolatry held sway all over the world. Everywhere there was fornication, adultery, licentiousness; everywhere greed, robbery, bloodshed. When the world was filled with so many evils, when the good seed had not yet been sown, when the land had not been cleared, and there were briars, thistles and weeds everywhere, when no ploughing had been done, no furrow cut, how could Jesus speak of a harvest and say it was plentiful? Why did he speak thus of the gospel?

Why indeed, if not that with things in such a state, he was about to send out his apostles all over the world. Most likely they were bewildered and anxious; they probably asked themselves: How can we even open our mouths, let alone stand up and preach in front of huge crowds of people? How can eleven of us put the whole world to rights? Can we speak to the wise when we are ignorant, to soldiers when we are unarmed, to rulers when we are subjects, to people of many different languages, people of foreign nations and alien speech, when we have only one language? Who will tolerate us if no one can understand what we say?

It was to save them from the anxiety of such reasoning that the Lord called the gospel a harvest. It was almost as if he said: Everything is ready, all is prepared. I am sending you to harvest the ripe grain. You will be able to sow and reap on the same day. You must be like the farmer who rejoices when he goes out to gather in his crops. He looks happy and is glad of heart. His hard work and many difficulties forgotten, he hurries out eagerly to reap their reward, hastening to collect his annual returns. Nothing stands in the way, there is no obstacle anywhere, nor any uncertainty regarding the future. There will be no heavy rain, no hail or drought, no devastating legions of locusts. And since the farmer at harvest time fears no such disasters, the reapers set to work dancing and leaping for joy.

You must be like them when you go out into the world—indeed your joy must be very much greater. You also are to gather in a harvest—a harvest easily reaped, a harvest already there waiting for you. You have only to speak, not to labor. Lend me your tongue, and you will see the ripe grain gathered into the royal granary. And with this he sent them out, saying: *Remember that I am with you always, until the end of the world.*

(Last Homilies 10, 2-3: Bareille, t. 20, 562-564)

John Chrysostom (c.347-407) was born at Antioch and studied under Diodore of Tarsus, the leader of the Antiochene school of theology. After a period of great austerity as a hermit, he returned to Antioch where he was ordained deacon in 381 and priest in 386. From 386 to 397 it was his duty to preach in the principal church of the city, and his best homilies, which earned him the title "Chrysostomos" or "the golden-mouthed," were preached at this time. In 397 Chrysostom became patriarch of Constantinople, where his efforts to reform the court, clergy, and people led to his exile in 404 and finally to his death from the hardships imposed on him. Chrysostom stressed the divinity of Christ against the Arians and his full humanity against the Apollinarians, but he had no speculative bent. He was above all a pastor of souls, and was one of the most attractive personalities of the early Church.

Twelfth Sunday in Ordinary Time

Gospel: Matthew 10:26-33

Do not be afraid of those who kill the body.

Commentary: Augustine

Thanks be to that grain of wheat who freely chose to die and so be multiplied! Thanks be to God's only Son, our Lord and Savior Jesus Christ, for whom the enduring of our human death was not a thing to be scorned if it would make us worthy of his life! Mark how alone he was before his passing: his is the voice of the psalmist who said, *I am all alone until I depart from this place*—a solitary grain that nevertheless contained an immense fruitfulness, a capacity to be multiplied beyond measure.

How many other grains of wheat imitating the Lord's passion do we find to gladden our hearts when we celebrate the anniversaries of the martyrs! Many members has that one grain, all united by bonds of peace and charity under their one head, our Savior himself, and, as you know from having heard it so often, all of them form one single body. Their many voices can often be heard praying in the psalms through the voice of a single speaker calling on God as if all were calling together, because all are one in him.

Let us listen to their cry. In it we can hear the words of the martyrs who found themselves hard pressed, beset by danger from violent storms of hatred in this world, a danger not so much to their bodies which, after all, they would have to part with sometime, but rather to their faith. If they were to give way, if they should succumb either to the harsh tortures of their persecutors or to love of this present life, they would forfeit the reward promised them by the God who had taken away all ground for fear. Not only had he said: *Do not be afraid of those who kill the body but are unable to kill the soul;* he had also left them his own example. The precept he had enjoined on them he personally carried out, without attempting to evade the hands of those who scourged him, the blows of those who struck him, or the spittle of those who spat on him. Neither the crown of thorns pressed into his head nor the cross to which the soldiers nailed him encountered any resistance from him. None of these torments did he try to avoid. Though he himself was under no obligation to suffer them, he endured them for those who were, making his own person a remedy for the sick. And so the martyrs suffered, but they would certainly have failed the test without the presence of him who said: *Know that I am with you always, until the end of time.*

(Expositions of the Psalms 69, 1: CCL 39:930-931)

Augustine (354-430) was born at Thagaste in Africa and received a Christian education, although he was not baptized until 387. In 391 he was ordained priest and in 395 he became coadjutor bishop to Valerius of Hippo, whom he succeeded in 396. Augustine's theology was formulated in the course of his struggle with three heresies: Manichaeism, Donatism, and Pelagianism. His writings are voluminous and his influence on subsequent theology immense. He molded the thought of the Middle Ages down to the thirteenth century. Yet he was above all a pastor and a great spiritual writer.

Thirteenth Sunday in Ordinary Time

Gospel: Matthew 10:37-42

Whoever does not take up his cross and follow me is not worthy of me.

Commentary: Hilary of Poitiers

Christ commanded the apostles to leave everything in the world that they held most dear, adding: *Whoever does not take up his cross and follow me is not worthy of me.* For those who belong to Christ have crucified their lower nature with its sinful passions and desires. No one is worthy of him who refuses to take up his cross, that is to say, to share the Lord's passion, death, burial, and resurrection, and to follow him by living out the mystery of faith in the newly received grace of the Spirit.

Whoever finds his life will lose it, and whoever loses his life for my sake will find it. This means that thanks to the power of the word and the renunciation of past sins, temporal gains are death to the soul, and temporal losses salvation. Apostles must therefore take death into their new life and nail their sins to the Lord's cross. They must confront their persecutors with contempt for things present, holding fast to their freedom by a glorious confession of faith, and shunning any gain that would harm their souls. They should know that no power over their souls has been given to anyone, and that by suffering loss in this short life they will achieve immortality.

Whoever receives you receives me, and whoever receives me receives the one who sent me. Christ gives us all a love for his teaching and a disposition to treat our teachers with courtesy. Earlier he had shown the danger facing those who refused to receive the apostles by requiring these to shake the dust off their feet as a testimony against them; now he commends those who do receive the apostles, assuring them of a greater recompense than they might have expected for their hospitality, and he teaches that since he still acts as mediator, when we receive him God enters us through him because he comes from God. Thus whoever receives the apostles receives Christ, and whoever receives Christ receives God the Father, since what is received in the apostles is nothing else than what is received in Christ; nor is there anything in Christ but what is in God. Through this disposition of graces to receive the apostles is to receive God, because Christ is in them and God is in Christ.

(Commentary on Saint Matthew's Gospel
10, 25-27; SC 254, 246-251)

Hilary (315-367) was elected bishop of Poitiers in 353. Because of his struggles with the Arians and his treatise on the Trinity, for which he was exiled, he has been called "the Athanasius of the West." He also wrote a commentary on Saint Matthew's gospel and another on a selection of the psalms. His style is difficult and obscure and he makes much use of allegory.

Fourteenth Sunday
in Ordinary Time

Gospel: Matthew 11:25-30

I am gentle and humble in heart.

Commentary: Attributed to John Chrysostom

Our Master is always the same, gentle and benevolent. In his constant concern for our salvation, he says explicitly in the gospel just read to us: *Come, learn from me, for I am gentle and humble in heart.*

What great condescension on the part of the Creator! And yet the creature feels no shame! *Come, learn from me.* The Master came to console his fallen servants. This is how Christ treats us. He shows pity when a sinner deserves punishment. When the race that angers him deserves to be annihilated, he addresses the guilty ones in the kindly words: *Come, learn from me, for I am gentle and humble in heart.*

God is humble, and we are proud! The judge is gentle; the criminal arrogant! The potter speaks in lowered voice; the clay discourses in the tones of a king! *Come, learn from me, for I am gentle and humble in heart.* Our master carries a whip not to wound, but to heal us. Reflect upon his indescribable kindness. Who could fail to love a master who never strikes his servants? Who would not marvel at a judge who beseeches a condemned criminal? Surely the self-abasement of these words must astound you.

I am the Creator and I love my work. I am the sculptor and I care for what I have made. If I thought of my dignity, I should not rescue fallen humankind. If I failed to treat its incurable sickness with fitting remedies, it would never recover its strength. If I did not console it, it would die. If I did nothing but threaten it, it would perish. This is why I apply the salve of kindness to it where it lies. Compassionately I bend down very low in order to raise it up. No one standing erect can lift a fallen man without putting a hand down to him.

Come, learn from me, for I am gentle and humble in heart. I do not make a show of words; I have left you the proof of my deeds. You can see that I am gentle and humble in heart from what I have become. Consider my nature, reflect upon my dignity, and marvel at the condescension I have shown you. Think of where I came from, and of where I am as I speak to you. Heaven is my throne, yet I talk to you standing on the earth! I am glorified on high, but because I am long-suffering I am not angry with you, *for I am gentle and humble in heart.*

(Homily on Saint Bassus: Bareille, t. 4, 509-510)

Fifteenth Sunday in Ordinary Time

Gospel: Matthew 13:1-23 or 13:1-9

A sower went out to sow.

Commentary: Gregory the Great

Dearly beloved, the reading from the holy gospel about the sower requires no explanation, but only a word of warning. In fact the explanation has been given by Truth himself, and it cannot be disputed by a frail human being. However, there is one point in our Lord's exposition which you ought to weigh well. It is this. If I told you that the seed represented the word, the field the world, the birds the demons, and the thorns riches, you would perhaps be in two minds as to whether to believe me. Therefore the Lord himself deigned to explain what he had said, so that you would know that a hidden meaning is to be sought also in those passages which he did not wish to interpret himself.

Would anyone have believed me if I had said that thorns stood for riches? After all, thorns are piercing and riches pleasurable. And yet riches are thorns because thoughts of them pierce the mind and torture it. When finally they lure a person into sin, it is as though they were drawing blood from the wound they have inflicted.

According to another evangelist, the Lord spoke in this parable not simply of riches but of deceptive riches, and with good reason. Riches are deceptive because they cannot stay with us for long; they are deceptive because they are incapable of relieving our spiritual poverty. The only true riches are those that make us rich in virtue. Therefore, if you want to be rich, beloved, love true riches. If you aspire to the heights of real honor, strive to reach the kingdom of heaven. If you value rank and renown, hasten to be enrolled in the heavenly court of the angels.

Store up in your minds the Lord's words which you receive through your ears, for the word of the Lord is the nourishment of the mind. When his word is heard but not stored away in the memory, it is like

106

food which has been eaten and then rejected by an upset stomach. A person's life is despaired of if he cannot retain his food; so if you receive the food of holy exhortations, but fail to store in your memory those words of life which nurture righteousness, you have good reason to fear the danger of everlasting death.

Be careful, then, that the word you have received through your ears remains in your heart. Be careful that the seed does not fall along the path, for fear that the evil spirit may come and take it from your memory. Be careful that the seed is not received in stony ground, so that it produces a harvest of good works without the roots of perseverance. Many people are pleased with what they hear and resolve to undertake some good work, but as soon as difficulties begin to arise and hinder them they leave the work unfinished. The stony ground lacked the necessary moisture for the sprouting seed to yield the fruit of perseverance.

Good earth, on the other hand, brings forth fruit by patience. The reason for this is that nothing we do is good unless we also bear with equanimity the injuries done us by our neighbors. In fact, the more we progress, the more hardships we shall have to endure in this world; for when our love for this present world dies, its sufferings increase. This is why we see many people doing good works and at the same time struggling under a heavy burden of afflictions. They now shun earthly desires, and yet they are tormented by greater sufferings. But, as the Lord said, they bring forth fruit by patience, because, since they humbly endure misfortunes, they are welcomed when these are over into a place of rest in heaven.

(Forty Gospel Homilies 1, 15. 1-2, 4)

Gregory the Great (c.540-604), a Roman by birth, is one of the four great doctors of the Western Church. His great grandfather was Pope Felix III (483-492). After a brilliant secular career he became a monk, having turned his own house on the Clivus Scauri into a monastery dedicated to Saint Andrew. From c.578 to 585 he was in Constantinople as "apocrisiatarius," or papal nuncio, at the imperial court. His *Morals on Job* were conferences given at their request to the small bank of monks who accompanied him there. On 3 September 590 he was elevated to the see of Peter in succession to Pelagius II. Apart from Saint Leo the Great, Gregory is the only pope who has left examples of his preaching to the Roman people.

Sixteenth Sunday
in Ordinary Time

Gospel: Matthew 13:24-43 or 13:24-30

Let them grow together until the harvest.

Commentary: Gregory Palamas

T*he kingdom of heaven may be compared to a man who sowed good
seed in his field, but when all were asleep his enemy came and
sowed darnel among the wheat.*

Now as the Lord himself explains, the darnel is the offspring of the
evil one. They bear his mark because they behave the way he does:
they are seeds of his sowing, and his children by adoption. Harvest
time will be the end of the world, for although it began long since and
continues now through death, only then will all things come to an end.

The reapers are the angels, for they are, and will be especially at
that time, the servants of the King of heaven. As Scripture says: *Just
as the darnel is collected and burnt in the fire, so it will be at the end
of the world. The Son of Man,* who is also the Son of the Father Most
High, *will send his angels, and they will gather out of his kingdom all
evildoers and every cause of sin.*

And so the Lord's servants, the angels of God, seeing the darnel in
the field, that is, wicked and impious folk living among good people,
and that even within the Church, said to the Lord: *Do you wish us to
go and gather it up?* In other words, "Shall we kill them, to remove
them from the earth?" But the Lord's reply was: *No, for fear that in
collecting the darnel you may also uproot the wheat.*

How then would the wheat, the good people, be uprooted as well if
the angels gathered up the darnel, cutting off the wicked by death to
separate them from the just? The fact is that many godless sinners who
live among people who are upright and devout repent in time and are
converted, and by learning new habits of piety and virtue they cease

to be darnel and become wheat. And so some wheat would be uprooted in the gathering of the darnel if the angels snatched the wicked away before they repented. Moreover, many while living evil lives produce children of good disposition, or they may have other rightly disposed descendants. This is why he who sees everything before it comes into being would not permit the darnel to be uprooted until the appointed time. But he says: *At harvest time I will say to the reapers: "First collect the darnel and bind it in bundles to be burnt, but gather the wheat into my barn."*

Those therefore who wish to be saved from eternal punishment and to inherit the everlasting kingdom of God must be not darnel but wheat. They must avoid saying or doing anything evil or useless, and practice the opposite virtues, thus bringing forth the fruits of repentance. In this way they will become worthy of the heavenly granary; they will be called children of the Father Most High, and as heirs will enter his kingdom rejoicing, resplendent with divine glory. To this may we all attain through the grace and loving kindness of our Lord Jesus Christ, to whom with his eternal Father and the most holy, good, and life-giving Spirit belongs glory now and always and for endless ages. Amen.

(Homily 27: PG 151, 346-354)

Gregory Palamas (1296-1359) was born at Constantinople, and prepared by the piety of his parents for a monastic vocation. At the age of about 20 he became a monk of Mount Athos. In 1347 he was made bishop of Thessalonica. Gregory stressed the biblical teaching that the human body and soul form a single united whole. On this basis he defended the physical exercises used by the Hesychasts in prayer, although he saw these only as a means to an end for those who found them helpful. He followed Saint Basil the Great and Saint Gregory of Nyssa in teaching that although no created intelligence can ever comprehend God in his essence, he can be directly experienced through his uncreated "energies," through which he manifests himself to and is present in the world. God's substance and his energies are distinct from one another, but they are also inseparable. One of these energies is the uncreated divine light, which was seen by the apostles on Mount Tabor. At times this is an inward illumination; at other times it is outwardly manifested.

Seventeenth Sunday in Ordinary Time

Gospel: Matthew 13:44-52 or 13:44-46

He sells everything he owns and buys the field.

Commentary: Origen

To the seeker after fine pearls may be applied the words, *Seek and you will find,* and, *Everyone who seeks will find.* If you ask what is to be sought, and what will be found by everyone who seeks for it, I say with all confidence: pearls—especially that pearl which will be acquired by those who give their all, who sacrifice everything for it, the pearl Paul meant when he said: *I have accepted the loss of everything in order to gain Christ. Everything* means beautiful pearls; *to gain Christ* refers to the one pearl of great price.

Admittedly, a lamp is precious to people in darkness, and they need it until sunrise. Precious too was the radiance on the face of Moses— and I believe on the faces of the other prophets also. It was a sight of beauty leading us to the point of being able to see the glory of Christ, to whom the Father bore witness in the words: *This is my beloved son, in whom I am well pleased.* But *compared with this surpassing glory, what formerly was glorious now seems to have no glory at all.* We need at first a glory destined to be outshone by an all-surpassing glory, just as we need the partial knowledge which *will be superseded when that which is perfect has come.*

Thus everyone beginning to live a spiritual life and growing toward maturity needs tutors, guardians, and trustees until the fullness of time arrives for him, so that after all this, he who at first was *no different from a slave although he owned the whole estate,* may on his emancipation receive his patrimony from his tutor, guardians, and trustees.

This patrimony is the pearl of great price, and the coming of what is perfect to supersede what is imperfect when, after acquiring the forms of knowledge, if we may call them so, which are inferior to knowledge of Christ, one becomes able to understand the supreme value of knowing Christ. The law and the prophets fully comprehended are the preparation for the full comprehension of the gospel and the complete understanding of the acts and words of Christ Jesus.

(Commentary on Matthew's Gospel 10, 9-10:
SC 162, 173-177)

Origen (183-253), one of the greatest thinkers of ancient times, became head of the catechetical school of Alexandria at the age of eighteen. In 230 he was ordained priest by the bishop of Caesarea. His life was entirely devoted to the study of Scripture and he was also a great master of the spiritual life. His book *On first Principles* was the first great theological synthesis. Many of his works are extant only in Latin as a result of his posthumous condemnation for heterodox teaching. Nevertheless, in intention he was always a loyal son of the Church.

Eighteenth Sunday in Ordinary Time

Gospel: Matthew 14:13-21

They all ate and were satisfied.

Commentary: Ephrem

Our Lord in a desert place changed a few loaves into many, and at Cana turned water into wine. Thus before the time came to give men and women his own body and blood to feed on, he accustomed their palates to his bread and wine, giving them a taste of transitory bread and wine to teach them to delight in his life-giving body and blood. He gave them things of little value for nothing to make them understand that his supreme gift would be given yet more freely. He gave them for nothing what they could have bought from him, what in fact they wanted to buy, to teach them that he asked them for no payment. When it was not permitted them to give him the price of bread and wine, which they could have done, they certainly could not pay him for his body and blood.

Moreover, as well as giving freely he lovingly cajoled us, offering us these small things without charge to attract us and cause us to go and receive something greater and beyond all price. He awakened our desire by things pleasing to the palate in order to draw us to that which gives life to the soul. He gave a sweet taste to the wine he created to show how great is the treasure hidden in his life-giving blood.

Consider how his creative power penetrates everything. Our Lord took a little bread, and in the twinkling of an eye multiplied it. Work that would take us ten months to accomplish he did with his ten fingers in a moment. His hands were as earth beneath the bread and his voice was as thunder above it. The movement of his lips acted as dew, the breath of his mouth as sunlight, and in a brief moment he accomplished what normally takes much time. Thus the shortage was forgotten;

many loaves came from few as in the first blessing: *Be fruitful and multiply and fill the earth.*

The Lord also showed those to whom he gave his precepts the power of his holy word, and how swiftly he would reward those who accepted it. Nevertheless, he did not increase the number of loaves as much as he could have done, but only enough to satisfy those who were to eat them. His power was not the measure of his miracle, but the people's hunger. Had his miracle been measured by his power it would have been a victory beyond all measure. Measured by the hunger of thousands, there was a surplus of twelve baskets full. Humans who practice any craft always fall short of their customers' desires—they are unable to meet their requirements; but what God does goes beyond anyone's desire. The Lord said: *Gather up what remains so that nothing is wasted* because he wanted to be sure they would not think they had seen a vision. When the fragments had been kept for a day or two they would believe the Lord had really done this, and they had not just imagined it.

(Diatessaron 12, 1. 3-5: CSCO 145
Scriptores Armeniaci, t. 2, 115-117)

Ephrem (c.306-373), the only Syrian Father who is honored as a doctor of the Church, was ordained deacon at Edessa in 363, and gave an outstanding example of a deacon's life and work. Most of his exegetical, dogmatic, controversial, and ascetical writings are in verse. They provide a rich mine of information regarding the faith and practice of the early Syrian Church. The poetry of Ephrem greatly influenced the development of Syriac and Greek hymnography.

Nineteenth Sunday in Ordinary Time

Gospel: Matthew 14:22-33

Bid me come to you upon the water.

Commentary: Augustine

The gospel tells us how Christ the Lord walked upon the waters of the sea, and how the apostle Peter did the same until fear made him falter and lose confidence. Then he began to sink and emerged from the water only after calling on the Lord with renewed faith.

Now we must regard the sea as a symbol of the present world, and the apostle Peter as a symbol of the one and only Church. For Peter, who ranked first among the apostles and was always the most ready to declare his love for Christ, often acted as spokesman for them all. For instance, when the Lord Jesus Christ asked who people thought he was and the other disciples had cited various opinions, it was Peter who responded to the Lord's further question, *But who do you say I am?* with the affirmation: *You are the Christ, the Son of the living God.* One replied for all because all were united.

When we consider Peter as a representative member of the Church we should distinguish between what was due to God's action in him and what was attributable to himself. Then we ourselves shall not falter; then we shall be founded upon rock and remain firm and unmoved in the face of the wind, rain, and floods, which are the trials and temptations of this present world. Look at Peter, who in this episode is an image of ourselves; at one moment he is all confidence, at the next all uncertainty and doubt; now he professes faith in the immortal One, now he fears for his life.

Lord, if it is you, bid me come to you upon the water. When the Lord said *Come* Peter climbed out of the boat and began to walk on the water. This is what he could do through the power of the Lord; what

114

by himself? *Realizing how violently the wind was blowing, he lost his nerve, and as he began to sink he called out, "Lord, I am drowning, save me"!* When he counted on the Lord's help it enabled him to walk on the water; when human frailty made him falter he turned once more to the Lord, who immediately stretched out his hand to help him, raised him up as he was sinking, and rebuked him for his lack of faith.

Think, then, of this world as a sea, whipped up to tempestuous heights by violent winds. A person's own private tempest will be his or her unruly desires. If you love God you will have power to walk upon the waters, and all the world's swell and turmoil will remain beneath your feet. But if you love the world it will surely engulf you, for it always devours its lovers, never sustains them. If you feel your foot slipping beneath you, if you become a prey to doubt or realize that you are losing control, if, in a word, you begin to sink, say: *Lord, I am drowning, save me!* Only he who for your sake died in your fallen nature can save you from the death inherent in that fallen nature.

(Sermon 76:1. 4. 5. 8. 9: PL 38, 479-483)

Augustine (354-430) was born at Thagaste in Africa and received a Christian education, although he was not baptized until 387. In 391 he was ordained priest and in 395 he became coadjutor bishop to Valerius of Hippo, whom he succeeded in 396. Augustine's theology was formulated in the course of his struggle with three heresies: Manichaeism, Donatism, and Pelagianism. His writings are voluminous and his influence on subsequent theology immense. He molded the thought of the Middle Ages down to the thirteenth century. Yet he was above all a pastor and a great spiritual writer.

Twentieth Sunday in Ordinary Time

Gospel: Matthew 15:21-28

Woman, you have great faith.

Commentary: John Chrysostom

The Canaanite woman whose daughter was tormented by a devil came to Christ begging his help. Most urgently she cried out: *Lord, have pity on me. My daughter is grievously tormented by a devil.* Notice that the woman was a foreigner, a gentile, a person from outside the Jewish community. What was she then but a dog, unworthy to obtain her request? *It is not fair, said the Lord, to take the children's bread and give it to the dogs.* Nevertheless, by perseverance she became worthy; for Christ not only admitted her to the same noble rank as the children, dog though she was, but he also sent her away with high praise, saying: *Woman, you have great faith. Let it be as you desire.* Now when Christ says: *You have great faith,* you need seek no further proof of the woman's greatness of soul. You see that an unworthy woman became worthy by perseverance.

Now would you like proof that we shall gain more by praying ourselves than by asking others to pray for us? The woman cried out and *the disciples went to Christ and said: Give her what she wants—she is shouting after us.* And he said to them: *I was sent only to the lost sheep of the house of Israel.* But when the woman herself, still crying out, came to him and said: *That is true, sir, and yet the dogs eat what falls from their master's table,* then he granted her request, saying: *Let it be as you desire.*

Have you understood? When the disciples entreated him the Lord put them off, but when the woman herself cried out begging for this favor he granted it. And at the beginning, when she first made her request, he did not answer, but after she had come to him once, twice, and a third time, he gave her what she desired. By this he was teaching us that he had withheld the gift not to drive her away, but to make that woman's patience an example for all of us.

Now that we have learned these lessons, let us not despair even if we are guilty of sin and unworthy of any favor. We know that we can make ourselves worthy by perseverance.

(Homily on Phil 1:18, 12-13: Bareille 5, 495-496)

John Chrysostom (c.347-407) was born at Antioch and studied under Diodore of Tarsus, the leader of the Antiochene school of theology. After a period of great austerity as a hermit, he returned to Antioch where he was ordained deacon in 381 and priest in 386. From 386 to 397 it was his duty to preach in the principal church of the city, and his best homilies, which earned him the title "Chrysostomos" or "the golden-mouthed," were preached at this time. In 397 Chrysostom became patriarch of Constantinople, where his efforts to reform the court, clergy, and people led to his exile in 404 and finally to his death from the hardships imposed on him. Chrysostom stressed the divinity of Christ against the Arians and his full humanity against the Apollinarians, but he had no speculative bent. He was above all a pastor of souls, and was one of the most attractive personalities of the early Church.

Twenty-First Sunday in Ordinary Time

Gospel: Matthew 16:13-20

You are Peter; to you I will give the keys of the kingdom of heaven.

Commentary: Attributed to John Chrysostom

Peter was to be entrusted with the keys of the Church, or rather, he was entrusted with the keys of heaven; to him would be committed the whole people of God. The Lord told him: *Whatever you bind on earth shall be bound in heaven, and whatever you loose on earth shall be loosed in heaven.* Now Peter was inclined to be severe, so if he had also been impeccable what forbearance would he have shown toward those he instructed? His falling into sin was thus a providential grace to teach him from experience to deal kindly with others.

Just think who it was whom God permitted to fall into sin—Peter himself, the head of the apostles, the firm foundation, the unbreakable rock, the most important member of the Church, the safe harbor, the strong tower; Peter, who had said to Christ, *Even if I have to die with you I will never deny you;* Peter, who by divine revelation had confessed the truth: *You are the Christ, the Son of the living God.*

The gospel relates that on the night that Christ was betrayed Peter went indoors and was standing by the fire warming himself when a girl accosted him: *You too were with that man yesterday,* she said. But Peter answered: *I do not know the man.*

Just now you said: *Even if I have to die with you,* and now you deny him and say: *I do not know the man.* Oh Peter, is this what you promised? You were not tortured or scourged; at the words of a mere slip of a girl you took refuge in denial!

Again the girl said to him: *You too were with that man yesterday.* Again he answered: *I have no idea what man you mean.*

Who was it that spoke to you, causing you to make this denial? Not some important person but a woman, a doorkeeper, an outcast, a slave, someone of no account whatever. She spoke to you and you answered with a denial. What a strange thing—a girl, a prostitute, accosted Peter himself and disturbed his faith! Peter, the pillar, the rampart, could not bear the threat of a girl! She had but to speak and the pillar swayed, the rampart itself was shaken!

A third time she repeated: *You too were with that man yesterday,* but a third time he denied it. Finally Jesus looked at him, reminding him of his previous assertion. Peter understood, repented of his sin, and began to weep. Mercifully, however, Jesus forgave him his sin, because he knew that Peter, being a man, was subject to human frailty.

Now, as I said before, the reason God's plan permitted Peter to sin was because he was to be entrusted with the whole people of God, and sinlessness added to his severity might have made him unforgiving toward his brothers and sisters. He fell into sin so that remembering his own fault and the Lord's forgiveness, he also might forgive others out of love for them. This was God's providential dispensation. He to whom the Church was to be entrusted, he, the pillar of the churches, the harbor of faith, was allowed to sin; Peter, the teacher of the world, was permitted to sin, so that having been forgiven himself he would be merciful to others.

(On Saints Peter and Elijah: PG 50, 727-728)

Twenty-Second Sunday in Ordinary Time

Gospel: Matthew 16:21-27

Whoever wishes to come after me must deny himself.

Commentary: Augustine

If anyone wished to be a follower of mine, let him renounce himself and take up his cross and come after me.

Our Lord's command seems hard and heavy, that anyone who wants to follow him must renounce himself. But no command is hard and heavy when it comes from one who helps to carry it out. That other saying of his is true: *My yoke is easy and my burden light.* Whatever is hard in his commands is made easy by love.

We know what great things love can accomplish, even though it is often base and sensual. We know what hardships people have endured, what intolerable indignities they have borne to attain the object of their love. What we love indicates the sort of people we are, and therefore making a decision about this should be our one concern in choosing a way of life. Why be surprised if people who set their hearts on Christ and want to follow him renounce themselves out of love? If we lose ourselves through self-love we must surely find ourselves through self-renunciation.

Who would not wish to follow Christ to supreme happiness, perfect peace, and lasting security? We shall do well to follow him there, but we need to know the way. The Lord Jesus had not yet risen from the dead when he gave this invitation. His passion was still before him; he had still to endure the cross, to face outrages, reproaches, scourging; to be pierced by thorns, wounded, insulted, taunted, and put to death. The road seems rough, you draw back, you do not want to follow Christ. Follow him just the same. The road we made for ourselves is rough, but Christ has leveled it by passing over it himself.

120

Who does not desire to be exalted? Everyone enjoys a high position. But self-abasement is the step that leads to it. Why take strides that are too big for you—do you want to fall instead of going up? Begin with this step and you will find yourself climbing. The two disciples who said: *Lord, command that one of us shall sit at your right hand in your kingdom and the other at your left* had no wish to think about this step of self-abasement. They wanted to reach the top without noticing the step that led there. The Lord showed them the step, however, by his reply: *Can you drink the cup that I am to drink?* You who aim at the highest exaltation, can you drink the cup of humiliation? He did not simply give the general command: *Let him renounce himself and follow me* but added: *Let him take up his cross and follow me.*

What does it mean to take up one's cross? It means bearing whatever is unpleasant—that is following me. Once you begin to follow me by conforming your life to my commandments, you will find many to contradict you, forbid you, or dissuade you, and some of these will be people calling themselves followers of Christ. Therefore if you meet with threats, flattery, or opposition, let this be your cross; pick it up and carry it—do not collapse under it. These words of our Lord are like an exhortation to endure martyrdom. If you are persecuted you ought, surely, to make light of any suffering for the sake of Christ.

(Sermon 96, 1-4: PL 38, 584-586)

Augustine (354-430) was born at Thagaste in Africa and received a Christian education, although he was not baptized until 387. In 391 he was órdained priest and in 395 he became coadjutor bishop to Valerius of Hippo, whom he succeeded in 396. Augustine's theology was formulated in the course of his struggle with three heresies: Manichaeism, Donatism, and Pelagianism. His writings are voluminous and his influence on subsequent theology immense. He molded the thought of the Middle Ages down to the thirteenth century. Yet he was above all a pastor and a great spiritual writer.

Twenty-Third Sunday in Ordinary Time

Gospel: Matthew 18:15-20

If your brother or sister listens to you, you will have won that person back.

Commentary: John Chrysostom

The Apostle says: *Whether you eat or drink, or whatever you do, do it all for the glory of God.*

You will be doing everything for the glory of God if, when you leave this place, you make yourselves responsible for saving a brother or sister, not just by accusing and rebuking him or her, but also by advising and encouraging, and by pointing out the harm done by worldly amusements, and the profit and help that come from our instruction. You will also be preparing for yourself a double reward, since as well as greatly furthering your own salvation, you will be endeavoring to heal a fellow member of Christ's body. It is the Church's pride, it is the Savior's command, not to be concerned only about our own welfare, but about our neighbor's also.

Think to what high honor you raise yourself when you regard someone else's salvation as a matter of extreme importance. As far as is humanly possible you imitate God himself, for listen to what he says through the prophet: "Whoever leads another from wrong to right *will be as my own mouth."* In other words, "Whoever tries to save those that are negligent, and to snatch them from the jaws of the devil, is imitating me as far as a human being can." What other work could equal this? Of all good deeds this is the greatest; of all virtue this is the summit.

And this is perfectly reasonable. Christ shed his own blood for our salvation; and Paul, speaking of those who give scandal and wound the consciences of people seeing them, cried out: *Because of your knowledge a weak brother or sister is destroyed—someone for whom Christ died!* So if your Lord shed his blood for that person, surely it is right for each of us to offer at least some words of encouragement and to extend a helping hand to those who through laxity have fallen into the snares of the devil.

But I am quite certain that you will do this out of the tender love you bear your own members, and that you will make every effort to bring your neighbors back to our common Mother, because I know that through the grace of God you are able to admonish others with wisdom.

(Homily 6, 18-20: SC 50, 224-225)

John Chrysostom (c.347-407) was born at Antioch and studied under Diodore of Tarsus, the leader of the Antiochene school of theology. After a period of great austerity as a hermit, he returned to Antioch where he was ordained deacon in 381 and priest in 386. From 386 to 397 it was his duty to preach in the principal church of the city, and his best homilies, which earned him the title "Chrysostomos" or "the golden-mouthed," were preached at this time. In 397 Chrysostom became patriarch of Constantinople, where his efforts to reform the court, clergy, and people led to his exile in 404 and finally to his death from the hardships imposed on him. Chrysostom stressed the divinity of Christ against the Arians and his full humanity against the Apollinarians, but he had no speculative bent. He was above all a pastor of souls, and was one of the most attractive personalities of the early Church.

Twenty-Fourth Sunday in Ordinary Time

Gospel: Matthew 18:21-35

I tell you that you must forgive not seven times but seventy times seven.

Commentary: Augustine

The Lord puts the parable of the unforgiving debtor before us that we may learn from it. He has no desire for us to die, so he warns us: *This is how your heavenly Father will deal with you if you, any of you, fail to forgive your brother or sister from your heart.*

Take notice now, for clearly this is no idle warning. The fulfillment of this command calls for the most vigorous obedience. We are all in debt to God, just as other people are in debt to us. Is there anyone who is not God's debtor? Only a person in whom no sin can be found. And is there anyone who has no brother or sister in his debt? Only if there be someone who has never suffered any wrong. Do you think anyone can be found in the entire human race who has not in turn wronged another in some way, incurring a debt to that person? No, all are debtors, and have others in debt to them. Accordingly, God who is just has told you how to treat your debtor, because he means to treat his in the same way.

There are two works of mercy which will set us free. They are briefly set down in the gospel in the Lord's own words: *Forgive and you will be forgiven,* and *Give and you will receive.* The former concerns pardon, the latter generosity. As regards pardon he says: "Just as you want to be forgiven, so someone is in need of your forgiveness." Again, as regards generosity, consider when a beggar asks you for something that you are a beggar too in relation to God. When we pray we are all beggars before God. We are standing at the door of a great householder, or rather, lying prostrate, and begging with tears. We are longing to receive a gift—the gift of God himself.

What does a beggar ask of you? Bread. And you, what do you ask of God, if not Christ who said: *I am the living bread that has come down from heaven?* Do you want to be pardoned? Then pardon others. Forgive and you will be forgiven. Do you want to receive? Give and you will receive.

If we think of our sins, reckoning up those we have committed by sight, hearing, thought, and countless disorderly emotions, I do not know whether we can even sleep without falling into debt. And so, every day we pray; every day we beat upon God's ears with our pleas; every day we prostrate ourselves before him saying: *Forgive us our trespasses, as we also forgive those who trespass against us.* Which of our trespasses, all of them or only some? All, you will answer. Do likewise, therefore, with those who have offended you. This is the rule you have laid down for yourself, the condition you have stipulated. When you pray according to this pact and covenant you remember to say: *Forgive us, as we also forgive our debtors.*

(Sermon 83, 2. 4: PL 38, 515-516)

Augustine (354-430) was born at Thagaste in Africa and received a Christian education, although he was not baptized until 387. In 391 he was ordained priest and in 395 he became coadjutor bishop to Valerius of Hippo, whom he succeeded in 396. Augustine's theology was formulated in the course of his struggle with three heresies: Manichaeism, Donatism, and Pelagianism. His writings are voluminous and his influence on subsequent theology immense. He molded the thought of the Middle Ages down to the thirteenth century. Yet he was above all a pastor and a great spiritual writer.

Twenty-Fifth Sunday in Ordinary Time

Gospel: Matthew 20:1-16

Why are you jealous because I am generous?

Commentary: Augustine

The gospel story about the vineyard workers is appropriate to this time of year, the season of the earthly grape harvest. But there is also another harvest, the spiritual one, at which God rejoices in the fruits of *his* vineyard.

The kingdom of heaven is like a householder who went out to hire men to work in his vineyard. In the evening he gave orders for all to be paid, beginning with the last comers and ending with the first. Now why did he pay the last comers first? Will not everyone be rewarded at the same time? We read in another gospel passage how the king will say to those placed on his right hand: *Come, you whom my Father has blessed: take possession of the kingdom prepared for you from the foundation of the world.* If all, then, are to receive their wages together, how should we understand this statement about those who arrived at the eleventh hour being paid first, and those who had been working since daybreak being paid last? If I can say anything to further your understanding, thanks be to God. Give thanks to him who teaches you through me, for my own knowledge is not the source of my teaching.

To take an example, then, let us ask which of two workers receives his wages sooner, one who is paid after an hour, or one who is paid after twelve hours? Anyone will answer: "One who is paid after an hour." So also in our parable. All the workmen were paid at the same time, but because some were paid after an hour and others after twelve hours, the former, having had a shorter time to wait, may be said to have received their wages first.

The earliest righteous people like Abel and Noah, called as it were at the first hour, will receive the joy of resurrection at the same time as we do. So also will others who came later, Abraham, Isaac, and Jacob, and those contemporary with them, called as we may say at the third hour; Moses and Aaron and those called with them at the sixth hour; and after them the holy prophets, called at the ninth hour. At the end of the world all Christians, called at the eleventh hour, will receive the joy of resurrection together with those who went before them. All will be rewarded at the same time, but the first comers will have had the longest to wait. Therefore, if they receive their reward after a longer period and we after a shorter one, the fact that our reward is not delayed will make it seem as though we were receiving it first, even though we all receive it together.

In that great reward, then, we shall all be equal—the first to the last and the last to the first. For the denarius stands for eternal life, in which all will have the same share. Although through diversity of merit some will shine more brilliantly than others, in the possession of eternal life there will be equality. What is endless for all will not be longer for one and shorter for another. What has no bounds will have none either for you or for me. Those who lived chastely in the married state will have one kind of splendor; virgins will have another. The reward for good works will differ from the crown of martyrdom; but where eternal life is concerned there can be no question of more or less for anyone. Whatever may be the individual's degree of glory, each one will live in it eternally. This is the meaning of the denarius.

(*Sermon 87, 1. 4-6. PL 38, 530 533*)

Augustine (354-430) was born at Thagaste in Africa and received a Christian education, although he was not baptized until 387. In 391 he was ordained priest and in 395 he became coadjutor bishop to Valerius of Hippo, whom he succeeded in 396. Augustine's theology was formulated in the course of his struggle with three heresies: Manichaeism, Donatism, and Pelagianism. His writings are voluminous and his influence on subsequent theology immense. He molded the thought of the Middle Ages down to the thirteenth century. Yet he was above all a pastor and a great spiritual writer.

Twenty-Sixth Sunday in Ordinary Time

Gospel: Matthew 21:28-32

He went out moved by regret. The tax collectors and prostitutes will precede you into the kingdom of God.

Commentary: Clement of Alexandria

The doors are open for all who sincerely and wholeheartedly return to God; indeed, the Father is most willing to welcome back a truly repentant son or daughter. The result of true repentance, however, is that you do not fall into the same faults again, but utterly uproot from your souls the sins for which you consider yourself worthy of death. When these have been destroyed God will again dwell within you, since Scripture says that for the Father and his angels in heaven the festal joy and gladness at the return of one repentant sinner is great beyond compare. That is why the Lord cried out: *What I want is mercy, not sacrifice. I desire not the death of a sinner but his conversion. Even if your sins are like crimson wool I will make them as white as snow; even if they are blacker than night I will wash them as white as wool.*

Although only God has power to forgive sins and cancel transgressions, the Lord commands us also to forgive our repentant brothers and sisters every day. So if we who are evil know how to give good gifts, how much more generous must be the Father of mercies, the good Father of all consolation, who is full of compassion and mercy, and whose nature it is to be patient and await our conversion! Genuine conversion, however, means ceasing to sin without any backward glances.

God pardons what is past, then, but for the future we are each responsible for ourselves. By repenting we condemn our past misdeeds and beg forgiveness of the Father, the only one who can in his mercy undo what has been done, and wipe away our past sins with the dew of his Spirit. And so, if you are a thief and desire to be forgiven, steal no more. If you are a robber, return your gains with interest. If you have been a false witness, practice speaking the truth. If you are a perjurer, stop taking oaths. You must also curb all the other evil passions: anger, lust, grief, and fear. No doubt you will be unable all at once to root out passions habitually given way to, but this can be achieved by God's power, human prayers, the help of your brothers and sisters, sincere repentance, and constant practice.

(Homily on the Salvation of the Rich 39-40:
PG 9, 644-645)

Clement of Alexandria (c.150-215) was born at Athens of pagan parents. Nothing is known of his early life nor of the reasons for his conversion. He was the pupil and the assistant of Pantaenus, the director of the catechetical school of Alexandria, whom he succeeded about the year 200. In 202 Clement left Alexandria because of the persecution of Septimus Severus, and resided in Cappadocia with his pupil, Alexander, later bishop of Jerusalem. Clement may be considered the founder of speculative theology. He strove to protect and deepen faith by the use of Greek philosophy. Central in his teaching is his doctrine of the Logos, who as divine reason is the teacher of the world and its lawgiver. Clement's chief work is the trilogy, "Exhortation to the Greeks," "The Teacher," and "Miscellanies."

Twenty-Seventh Sunday in Ordinary Time

Gospel: Matthew 21:33-43

He leased his vineyard to other farmers.

Commentary: Basil the Great

You need only to look at the vine to be reminded of your own nature, that is, if you observe it intelligently. No doubt you remember the image used by the Lord in which he says that he is the vine and the Father the vinedresser. Each of us who have been grafted onto the Church by faith he calls branches, and he urges us to bear much fruit so as not to be rejected as useless and thrown onto the fire.

Throughout the Scriptures the Lord continually likens human souls to vines. He says for instance: *My beloved had a vineyard on a fertile hillside;* and again: *I planted a vineyard and put a hedge round it.* Clearly it is human souls that he calls his vineyard, and the hedge he has put round them is the security of his commandments and the protection of the angels; for *the angel of the Lord will encamp around those who fear him.* Moreover, by establishing in the Church apostles in the first place, prophets in the second, and teachers in the third, he has surrounded us as though by a firmly planted palisade.

In addition, the Lord has raised our thoughts to heaven by the examples of saints of past ages. He has kept them from sinking to the earth where they would deserve to be trampled on, and he wills that the bonds of love, like the tendrils of a vine, should attach us to our neighbors and make us rest on them, so that always climbing upward like vines growing on trees, we may reach the loftiest heights.

He also requires that we allow ourselves to be weeded. To be spiritually weeded means to have renounced the worldly ambitions that burdened our hearts. Anyone who has renounced the love of material things and attachment to possessions, or who has come to regard as despicable and deserving of contempt the poor, wretched glory of this world, is like a weeded vine. Freed from the profitless burden of earthly aspirations, that person can breathe again.

Finally, following out the implications of the comparison, we must not run to wood, or, in other words, show off or seek the praise of outsiders. Instead, we must bear fruit by reserving the display of our good works for the true vinedresser.

(Homilies on the Hexaemeron, 5: SC 27, 304-307)

Basil the Great (c.330-379), one of the three great Cappadocian Fathers, received an excellent education and began a career as a rhetorician before a spiritual awakening led him to receive baptism and become a monk. After visiting ascetics in Egypt, Palestine, Syria, and Mesopotamia, he decided that it was better for monks to live together in monasteries than alone as hermits, and he set about organizing Cappadocian monasticism. Basil's Rules influenced Saint Benedict. In 370 Basil succeeded Eusebius as bishop of Caesarea. His main concern was for the unity of the Church, and he strove to establish better relations between Rome and the East. His efforts bore fruit only after his death. Basil's writings include dogmatic, ascetic, and pedagogic treatises as well as letters and sermons.

Twenty-Eighth Sunday in Ordinary Time

Gospel: Matthew 22:1-14

Whomsoever you find invite to the wedding.

Commentary: Augustine

All believers are familiar with the story of the wedding of the king's son and the banquet that followed it, and of how the Lord's table was thrown open to all comers. When everyone was seated *the master of the house came in to see his guests, and among them he noticed one without a wedding garment. So he said to him, "My friend, how did you get in here without a wedding garment?"*

Now what precisely does this mean? Let us try to find out what it is that some believers have, but which the wicked lack, for that will be what the wedding garment is.

Can it be one of the sacraments? Hardly, for these, as we know, are common to good and bad alike. Take baptism for example. It is true that no one comes to God except through baptism, but not every baptized person comes to him. We cannot take this sacrament as the wedding garment, then, for it is a robe worn not only by good people but also by wicked people. Perhaps, then, it is our altar that is meant, or at least what we receive from it. But we know that many who approach the altar eat and drink to their own damnation. Well, then, maybe it is fasting? The wicked can fast too. What about going to church? Some bad people also go to church.

Whatever can this wedding garment be, then? For an answer we must go to the Apostle, who says: *The purpose of our command is to arouse the love that springs from a pure heart, a clear conscience, and a genuine faith.* There is your wedding garment. It is not love of just any kind. Many people of bad conscience appear to love one another, but you will not find in them *the love that springs from a pure heart,*

132

a clear conscience, and a genuine faith. Only that kind of love is the wedding garment.

If I speak in the tongues of men and of angels, says the Apostle, *but have no love, I am nothing but a booming gong or a clashing cymbal. If I have the gift of prophecy, if I have all knowledge and understand all mysteries, if I have faith strong enough to move mountains, but have no love, I am nothing.* In other words, even with all these gifts I am nothing without Christ. Does that mean that prophecy has no value and that knowledge of mysteries is worthless? No, they are not worthless but I am, if I possess them but have no love. But can the lack of one good thing rob so many others of their value? Yes, without love my confession of the name of Christ even by shedding my blood or offering my body to be burnt will avail me nothing, for I may do this out of a desire for glory. That such things can be endured for the sake of empty show without any real love for God the Apostle also declares. Listen to him: *If I give away all I have to the poor, if I hand over my body to be burnt, but have no love, it will avail me nothing.* So this is what the wedding garment is. Examine yourselves to see whether you possess it. If you do, your place at the Lord's table is secure.

(Sermon 90, 1. 5-6: PL 38, 559. 561-563)

Augustine (354-430) was born at Thagaste in Africa and received a Christian education, although he was not baptized until 387. In 391 he was ordained priest and in 395 he became coadjutor bishop to Valerius of Hippo, whom he succeeded in 396. Augustine's theology was formulated in the course of his struggle with three heresies: Manichaeism, Donatism, and Pelagianism. His writings are voluminous and his influence on subsequent theology immense. He molded the thought of the Middle Ages down to the thirteenth century. Yet he was above all a pastor and a great spiritual writer.

Twenty-Ninth Sunday
in Ordinary Time

Gospel: Matthew 22:15-21

Give to Ceasar the things that are Caesar's and to God the things that are God's.

Commentary: Lawrence of Brindisi

In today's gospel we find two questions: one put to Christ by the Pharisees, and the other put by him to them. The Pharisees' question concerns this world alone, while Christ's has an entirely heavenly and other-worldly sense. Their question derived from profound ignorance and perversity; his stemmed from perfect wisdom and goodness.

Whose likeness and inscription is this? Caesar's, they reply. *Then give to Caesar the things that are Caesar's, and to God the things that are God's.* To each, he says, must be given what belongs to him. This, surely, is a judgment full of heavenly wisdom and instruction. For it teaches that authority is twofold, having an earthly and human aspect, and a heavenly and divine aspect. It teaches that we owe a twofold duty of obedience: to human laws and to the law of God. The coin bearing Caesar's likeness and inscription must be given to Caesar, and the one stamped with the divine image and likeness must be given to God. *We bear the imprint of your glorious face, O Lord.*

We are made *in the image and likeness of God.* So you, O Christian, because you are a human being, are God's tribute money—a little coin bearing the image and likeness of the divine emperor. Therefore with Christ I ask, *Whose likeness and inscription is this?* Your answer is, God's. To which I reply, Then why not give God what belongs to him?

If we really want to be God's image, we must be like Christ, for his is the image of God's goodness and *the perfect copy of his nature,* and God *foreordained that those he has chosen should take on a likeness to his son.* Christ undoubtedly gave Caesar what was Caesar's and

God what was God's. He fulfilled to perfection the precepts of both tablets of the law, becoming *obedient unto death, even death on a cross,* and he was most highly endowed, both inwardly and outwardly, with every virtue.

In today's gospel the reply, most wise and discreet, by which Christ sidestepped his enemies' trap shows his great prudence. His teaching that each must be given what belongs to him, and also the example he gave by being willing to pay the temple tax and giving a shekel for himself and Peter, shows his justice. His declaring it to be a duty to pay taxes to Caesar, openly teaching the truth without fear of the Jews who would be offended, shows his fortitude. For this is God's way, of which Christ is the authentic teacher.

Those therefore who resemble Christ in their lives, conduct, and practice of the virtues, they are the ones who truly manifest the divine image; for the way to recover this image is by being absolutely just. *Give to Caesar the things that are Caesar's, and to God the things that are God's;* that is, give each what belongs to him.

(Opera omnia 8, 335. 336. 339-340. 346)

Lawrence of Brindisi (1559-1619) was born at Brindisi and educated at Venice. In 1575 he entered with the Capuchins and was sent to Padua to study philosophy and theology. He had a prodigious memory and was said to know the Scriptures by heart in the original. This enabled him to convert many Jews. Raised to a high degree of contemplation himself, he evangelized much of Europe, speaking to the hearts of those who heard him. From 1602 he served a term as minister general of the Capuchins. As chaplain to the imperial troops he led them into battle and to victory against the Turks on two occasions, armed only with a crucifix. He died at Lisbon while on an embassy. His writings include eight volumes of sermons, commentaries on Genesis and Ezekiel, and other didactic or controversial works. Pope John XXIII added his name to the list of Doctors of the Church.

Thirtieth Sunday
in Ordinary Time

Gospel: Matthew 22:34-40

You shall love the Lord your God and your neighbor as yourself.

Commentary: Augustine

I know, beloved, how well fed you are every day by the exhortations of Holy Scripture, and what nourishment your hearts find in the word of God. Nevertheless, the affection we have for one another compels me to say something to you, beloved, about love. What else is there to speak of apart from love? To speak about love there is no need to select some special passage of Scripture to serve as a text for the homily; open the Bible at any page and you will find it extolling love. We know this is so from the Lord himself, as the gospel reminds us, for when asked what were the most important commandments of the law he answered: *You shall love the Lord your God with all your heart, and with all your soul, and with all your mind; and you shall love your neighbor as yourself.* And then, just in case you might be tempted to search further through the pages of Holy Scripture for some commandments other than these two, he added: *The entire law and the prophets also depend upon these two commandments.* If the entire law and the prophets depend upon these two commandments, how much more must the gospel do so?

People are renewed by love. As sinful desire ages them, so love rejuvenates them. Enmeshed in the toils of his desires the psalmist laments: *I have grown old surrounded by my enemies.* Love, on the other hand, is the sign of our renewal as we know from the Lord's own words: *I give you a new commandment—love one another.*

Even in former times there were people who loved God without thought of reward, and whose hearts were purified by their chaste longing for him. They drew back the veils obscuring the ancient promises, and caught a glimpse through these figures of a new covenant to come. They saw that all the precepts and promises of the old covenant, geared to the capacities of an unregenerate people, prefigured a new covenant which the Lord would bring to fulfillment in the last age. The Apostle says this quite clearly: *The things that happened to them were symbolic, and were recorded for us who are living in the last age.* When the time for it came the new covenant began to be openly proclaimed, and those ancient figures were expounded and explained so that all might understand that the old covenant promises pointed to the new covenant.

And so love was present under the old covenant just as it is under the new, though then it was more hidden and fear was more apparent, whereas now love is more clearly seen and fear is diminished. For as love grows stronger we feel more secure, and when our feeling of security is complete fear vanishes, since, as the apostle John declares: *Perfect love casts out fear.*

(Sermon 350A, 1-2: PLS 2, 449-450)

Augustine (354-430) was born at Thagaste in Africa and received a Christian education, although he was not baptized until 387. In 391 he was ordained priest and in 395 he became coadjutor bishop to Valerius of Hippo, whom he succeeded in 396. Augustine's theology was formulated in the course of his struggle with three heresies: Manichaeism, Donatism, and Pelagianism. His writings are voluminous and his influence on subsequent theology immense. He molded the thought of the Middle Ages down to the thirteenth century. Yet he was above all a pastor and a great spiritual writer.

Thirty-First Sunday in Ordinary Time

Gospel: Matthew 23:1-12

They do not practice what they preach.

Commentary: Paschasius Radbertus

Christ is called master, or teacher, by right of nature rather than by courtesy, for all things subsist through him. Through his incarnation and life upon earth we are taught the way to eternal life. Our reconciliation with God is dependent on the fact of his being greater than we are. Yet, having told his disciples not to allow themselves to be called master, or to love seats of honor and things of that kind, he himself set an example and was a model of humility. It is as though he said: Even as *I do not seek my own glory (though there is One who seeks it),* so neither must you love to be honored above others, or to be called master. Look at me: *The Son of Man did not come to be served but to serve, and to give his life for many.*

This was said not only for the instruction of his disciples, but also of those who are teachers in the Church. None of them must seek positions of honor; whoever wishes to be greater than the rest must first become the servant of all, as Christ himself did. If anyone wants a high office let him want the labor it entails, not the honor it will bring him. He should desire to serve and minister to everyone, and not expect everyone to serve and minister to him. For the desire to be served comes from the supercilious attitude of the Pharisees; the desire to serve from the teaching of Christ. Those who canvass for positions of honor are the ones who exalt themselves; and similarly it is those who of their own accord humble themselves who will be exalted by the Lord.

After specifically reserving the office of teaching to himself, Christ immediately went on to give as the rule of his teaching that whoever wants to be greatest should be the servant of all. And he gave the same rule in other words when he said: *Learn of me, for I am meek and humble of heart.* Anyone therefore who wants to be Christ's disciple must hasten to learn the lesson he professes to teach, for a perfect disciple will be like his master. Otherwise, if he refuses to learn the master's lesson, far from being a master himself, he will not even be a disciple.

(Commentary on Saint Matthew's Gospel
10, 23: PL 120, 769-770)

Paschasius Radbertus (c.785-860) was brought up by the nuns of Notre Dame at Soissons, after being left abandoned on their doorstep. He received the monastic habit at Corbie, and was the confidant of two successive abbots. On the death of Abbot Wala Paschasius himself became abbot, but he found the office uncongenial and resigned after seven years. He always refused to be raised to the priesthood. Paschasius, who was a prolific writer, is noted especially for the part he played in establishing the Catholic doctrine on the eucharist. He also wrote lengthy commentaries on Matthew and on the forty-fourth psalm.

Thirty-Second Sunday
in Ordinary Time

Gospel: Matthew 25:1-13

Look, the bridegroom comes. Go out to meet him.

Commentary: Attributed to Anthony

B*lessed are the pure in heart, for they shall see God,* since purity of heart leads to perfection. Two things are contained within the heart—goodness which is natural to it and evil which is unnatural. This latter gives rise to such passions of the soul as murmuring, envy, detraction, and all the rest. Goodness, on the other hand, promotes knowledge of God and rids the soul of all these passions. If people honestly try to root out vice and avoid evil, if they repent with tears and sighs, devoting themselves humbly to a life of prayer, fasting, and watching, the Lord in his goodness will come to their aid and free them from all sinful inclinations.

Many who have lived a celibate monastic life for a long time have failed to learn what purity of heart is, because instead of studying the teaching of the fathers, they have followed their own wayward desires. So evil spirits and rebel marauders of the air have prevailed against them, hurling invisible darts by day and night, and thus preventing them from finding rest anywhere. Moreover they fill their hearts with pride, vanity, jealousy, criticism, raging anger, strife, and any number of other passions.

Such people are to be reckoned with the five foolish virgins because they have spent their time foolishly. They have not controlled their tongues nor cleansed their eyes and bodies from concupiscence, neither have they purged their hearts of lust and other deplorable defilements. It was enough for them merely to wear a woolen garment signifying virginity. Consequently they lack the heavenly joy which would kindle their lamps, and the Bridegroom does not open the door to them but repeats what he said to the foolish virgins: *Truly I say to you, I know you not.*

My only reason for writing you this letter is my desire for your salvation. I want you to be free and faithful and pure brides of Christ, the Bridegroom of all holy souls; as Saint Paul says: *I have espoused you to one husband that I may present you as a chaste bride to Christ.*

Let us awake, then, while we are still in this body, and grieve over ourselves, lamenting day and night from the bottom of our hearts, so that we may escape the bitter torment, the weeping, wailing, and remorse that will have no end. We must beware of entering through the wide gate and taking the easy road that leads to perdition, for many go that way. Instead we must enter by the narrow gate and take the path of sorrow and affliction that leads to life. Few people enter this gate, but those who do are real workers who will have the joy of receiving the reward of their labors and will inherit the kingdom.

If any are prepared to set out I do beg them not to delay and waste time, for they may be like the foolish virgins and find no one willing to sell them oil. These virgins burst into tears and cried out: *Lord, open to us.* But he answered: *Truly I say to you, I know you not.* And this happened to them simply because of their laziness.

I beg you by the grace of God to obey me as I also will obey you; and may we all obey the Lord who said by the tongue of the Prophet: *Who longs for life and desires to see good days? Keep your tongue from evil talk and your lips from deceitful speech. Turn away from evil and do good; seek and strive after peace.*

(Letter 20: PG 40, 1056-1058. 1061)

Thirty-Third Sunday in Ordinary Time

Gospel: Matthew 25:14-30

Because you have proved trustworthy in managing a small amount, come and share your master's joy.

Commentary: John Chrysostom

In the parable of the talents the Master entrusted money to his servants and then set out on a journey. This was to help us understand how patient he is, though in my view this story also refers to the resurrection. Here it is a question not of a vineyard and vine dressers, but of all workers. The Master is addressing everyone, not only rulers, or the Jews.

Those bringing him their profit acknowledge frankly what is their own, and what is their Master's. One says: *Sir, you gave me five talents;* another says; *You gave me two,* recognizing that they had received from him the means of making a profit. They are extremely grateful, and attribute to him all their success.

What does the Master say then? *Well done, good and faithful servant* (for goodness shows itself in concern for one's neighbor). *Because you have proved trustworthy in managing a small amount, I will give you charge of a greater sum: come and share your Master's joy.*

But one servant has a different answer. He says: *I knew you were a hard man, reaping where you have not sown and gathering where you have not winnowed; and I was afraid, and hid your talent. Here it is—you have back what belongs to you.*

What does the Master say to that? *You wicked servant! You should have put my money in the bank,* that is, "You should have spoken out and given encouragement and advice." "But no one will pay attention." "That is not your concern. You should have deposited the money" he says, "and left me to reclaim it, which I should have done with interest," meaning by interest the good works that are seen to follow the hearing of the word. "The easier part is all you were expected to do, leaving the harder part to me." Because the servant failed to do this, the Master said: *Take the talent away from him, and give it to the servant who has the ten talents. For to everyone who has more will be given, and he will have enough and to spare; but the one who has not will forfeit even the little he has.*

What is the meaning of this? That whoever has received for the good of others the ability to preach and teach, and does not use it, will lose that ability, whereas the zealous servant will be given greater ability, even as the other forfeits what he had.

(Homily 78 on Saint Matthew's Gospel:
Bareille, t. 13, 93-94)

John Chrysostom (c.347-407) was born at Antioch and studied under Diodore of Tarsus, the leader of the Antiochene school of theology. After a period of great austerity as a hermit, he returned to Antioch where he was ordained deacon in 381 and priest in 386. From 386 to 397 it was his duty to preach in the principal church of the city, and his best homilies, which earned him the title "Chrysostomos" or "the golden-mouthed," were preached at this time. In 397 Chrysostom became patriarch of Constantinople, where his efforts to reform the court, clergy, and people led to his exile in 404 and finally to his death from the hardships imposed on him. Chrysostom stressed the divinity of Christ against the Arians and his full humanity against the Apollinarians, but he had no speculative bent. He was above all a pastor of souls, and was one of the most attractive personalities of the early Church.

Christ the King
Thirty-Fourth Sunday in Ordinary Time

Gospel: Matthew 25:31-46

The Son of Man will take his seat on his throne of glory and will separate
people from one another.

Commentary: Hippolytus

As the holy gospel clearly proclaims, the Son of Man will gather
together all nations. *He will separate people one from another,
as a shepherd separates sheep from goats. The sheep he will place at
his right hand, the goats at his left. Then he will say to those at his
right: Come, my Father's blessed ones, inherit the kingdom prepared
for you from the foundation of the world.* Come, you lovers of poor
people and strangers. Come, you who fostered my love, for I am love.
Come, you who shared peace, for I am peace.

*Come, my Father's blessed ones, inherit the kingdom prepared for
you* who did not make an idol of wealth, who gave alms to the poor,
help to orphans and widows, drink to the thirsty, and food to the
hungry. Come, you who welcomed strangers, clothed the naked,
visited the sick, comforted prisoners, and assisted the blind. Come,
you who kept the seal of faith unbroken, who were swift to assemble
in the churches, who listened to my Scriptures, longed for my words,
observed my law day and night, and like good soldiers shared in my
suffering because you wanted to please me, your heavenly King.
*Come, inherit the kingdom prepared for you from the foundation of
the world.* Look, my kingdom is ready, paradise stands open, my
immortality is displayed in all its beauty. Come now, all of you, *inherit
the kingdom prepared for you from the foundation of the world.*

Then, astounded at so great a wonder—at being addressed as
friends by him whom the angelic hosts are unable clearly to behold—
the righteous will reply, exclaiming: *Lord, when did we see you hungry*

and feed you? Master, *when did we see you thirsty and give you a drink? When did we see you,* whom we hold in awe, *naked and clothe you? When did we see you,* the immortal One, *a stranger and welcome you? When did we see you,* lover of our race, *sick or in prison and come to visit you?* You are the Eternal, without beginning like the Father, and co-eternal with the Spirit. You are the One who created all things from nothing; you are the King of angels; you make the depths tremble; you *are clothed in light as in a robe;* you are our maker who fashioned us from the earth; you are the creator of the world invisible. The whole earth flies from your presence. How could we possibly have received your lordship, your royal majesty, as our guest?

Then will the King of Kings say to them in reply: *Inasmuch as you did this to one of the least of these my brothers and sisters, you did it to me.* Inasmuch as you received, clothed, fed, and gave a drink to those members of mine about whom I have just spoken to you, that is, to the poor, you did it to me. So come, enter *the kingdom prepared for you from the foundation of the world;* enjoy for ever the gift of my heavenly Father, and of the most holy and life-giving Spirit. What tongue can describe those blessings? *Eye has not seen, nor ear heard, nor human heart conceived what God has prepared for those who love him.*

*(The Consummation of the World
and the Anti-Christ 41-43: PG 10, 944-945)*

Hippolytus (c.170-236) was a Roman priest who probably came originally from the East. When Pope Callistus relaxed the penitential discipline of the Church, Hippolytus became the first anti-pope. The schism continued into the reign of Pontianus, but when Pontianus and Hippolytus were both exiled to the mines of Sardinia they were reconciled before dying as martyrs for the faith.

Presentation of the Lord

Gospel: Luke 2:22-40 or 2:22-32

My eyes have seen your saving power.

Commentary: Origen

Let us reflect upon the way everything was prearranged for Simeon to embrace the Son of God. In the first place, he had been given a revelation by the Holy Spirit that *he would not die before he had seen the Lord's Anointed.* Then, he did not enter the temple by chance or routine, but he came there under the prompting of the Spirit of God, *for all who are led by the Spirit of God are children of God.* If you too wish to embrace Jesus and enfold him in your arms, strive with all your might to follow the guidance of the Spirit and come to God's temple. Now, at this moment, you are standing in the temple of the Lord Jesus, which is his Church, the temple built of living stones. When your life and conduct are really worthy of the name of Church, you are standing in the Lord's temple.

If, led by the Spirit, you come to the temple, you will find the child Jesus, you will lift him up in your arms and say: *Now, Lord, you let your servant go in peace as you promised.* Notice at once that peace is joined to death and dismissal, for Simeon does not say only that he wishes to go, but adds that he wished to go in peace. This is the same promise as was made to blessed Abraham: *You shall go to your ancestors in peace when you have reached a ripe old age.* Who dies in peace? Only the person who has *the peace of God which passes all understanding,* and which guards the heart of its possessor. Who departs from this world in peace? Only the person who understands that *God was reconciling the world to himself in Christ,* and who, being in no way at enmity with God or opposed to him, has acquired complete peace and concord through good works, and so is allowed like Abraham to go in peace and join the holy patriarchs.

But why speak of the patriarchs? Shall I not rather go on to speak about Jesus, the prince and lord of patriarchs, about whom Saint Paul says: *It is better to die and be with Christ?* That person possesses Jesus who dares to say: *It is no longer I who live—it is Christ who lives in me.*

And so, as we stand in the temple and hold the Son of God and embrace him, let us pray to almighty God and to the child Jesus that we may be found worthy of discharge and departure to better things, for we long to speak with Jesus and embrace him. To him be glory and power forever and ever. Amen.

(Homily XV on Luke: SC 87, 2344-2346)

Origen (183-253), one of the greatest thinkers of ancient times, became head of the catechetical school of Alexandria at the age of eighteen. In 230 he was ordained priest by the bishop of Caesarea. His life was entirely devoted to the study of Scripture and he was also a great master of the spiritual life. His book *On first Principles* was the first great theological synthesis. Many of his works are extant only in Latin as a result of his posthumous condemnation for heterodox teaching. Nevertheless, in intention he was always a loyal son of the Church.

Birth of Saint John the Baptist

Gospel: Luke 1:57-60.80

John is his name.

Commentary: Bede

Quite rightly does the universal Church, which celebrates the many triumphs by which the holy martyrs gained entry into heaven, honor also the birth of Saint John the Baptist and his alone, apart from that of our Lord. We may be certain that this custom did not arise without the support of the gospel. On the contrary, we should treasure in our hearts the fact that as an angel appeared to the shepherds when our Lord was born and said: *Behold, I bring you good news of a great joy which will come to all the people; for to you is born this day a savior, who is Christ the Lord,* so also an angel told Zechariah that John would be born, adding: *You will have joy and gladness, and many will rejoice at his birth, for he will be great before the Lord.* With good reason is the birth of each celebrated with joy and devotion, but in the one case joy is proclaimed to all peoples at the birth of Christ the Lord, the Savior of the world, the Son of almighty God, the Sun of Righteousness, while in the other case it is recounted that many will rejoice at the appearance of the Lord's forerunner, his mighty servant, a blazing and radiant lamp.

John went ahead in the spirit and power of Elijah to teach the Lord's people to be perfect, baptizing them with water so that they would be able to accept Christ when he appeared. Christ came after John in the spirit and power of God the Father to make it possible for them to be perfect, baptizing them with the Holy Spirit and with fire so that they would be able to see the face of the Father.

It is significant that John's birth is recorded as having taken place when the days began to grow shorter, while the Lord was born as they grew longer. It was John himself who explained the meaning of this contrast when the crowd thought he was the Christ because of his great virtues, and the Lord was considered by some as only a prophet and not the Christ because of his lack of austerity. *He must increase,* said John, *while I must decrease.* The Lord did indeed increase because his followers throughout the world came to know that he who had been reputed a prophet was in fact the Christ. John decreased and was ranked lower because whereas he had been considered the Christ, it became apparent that he was not Christ himself but his herald. So it was fitting that after John's birth the days should begin to grow shorter, for the rumor that he was divine would die away and his baptism would shortly come to an end. Rightly, too, when the Lord was born the short winter day started to draw out, for he had appeared who was going to shed on all races the light of his knowledge, of which previously only the Jews had had but a partial possession, and spread the warmth of his love over the whole wide world.

(Homily II, 20: CCL 122, 328-330)

Bede (c.673-735), who received the title of Venerable less than a century after his death, was placed at the age of seven in the monastery of Wearmouth, then ruled by Saint Benet Biscop. From there he was sent to Jarrow, probably at the time of its foundation in about 681. At the age of 30 he was ordained priest. His whole life was devoted to the study of Scripture, to teaching, writing, and the prayer of the Divine Office. He was famous for his learning, although he never went beyond the bounds of his native Northumbria. Bede is best known for his historical works, which earned him the title "Father of English History." His *Historia Ecclesiastica Gentis Anglorum* is a primary source for early English history, especially valuable because of the care he took to give his authorities, and to separate historical fact from hearsay and tradition. In 1899 Bede was proclaimed a doctor of the Church.

Saints Peter and Paul

Gospel: Matthew 16:13-19

You are Peter, and I will give you the keys of the kingdom of heaven.

Commentary: Aelred of Rievaulx

You know, brethren, that of all our Lord's apostles and martyrs the two whose feast we celebrate today seem to possess a special grandeur. Nor is this surprising, since to these two men the Lord entrusted his Church in a special way. For when Saint Peter proclaimed that the Lord was the Son of God, the Lord told him: *You are Peter, and on this rock I will build my Church. And I will give you the keys of the kingdom of heaven.* But in a way the Lord put Saint Paul on the same level, as Paul himself said: *He who worked through Peter in the apostolate also worked through me among the Gentiles.*

These are the men whom the Lord promised to the Church when he said through the prophet: *In place of your fathers, sons are born to you.* The fathers of the Church are the holy patriarchs and prophets who first taught the law of God and foretold the coming of our Lord. Our Lord came, and to replace the prophets he chose the holy apostles, thus fulfilling what the prophet had said: *In place of your fathers, sons are born to you.* See, moreover, how he shows the responsibility of the apostles to be greater than that of the prophets. The prophets were leaders of a single people and lived in a single nation and one part of the world, whereas he said of the apostles: *You will make them princes over all the earth.* And indeed, brethren, is there any place on earth that has not seen the power and grandeur of these apostles?

These are the pillars that support the Church by their teaching, their prayers, their example of patience. Our Lord strengthened these pillars. In the beginning they were very weak and could not support either themselves or others. This had been wonderfully arranged by our Lord, for if they had always been strong, one might have thought their strength was their own. Our Lord wished to show first what they were of themselves and only afterwards to strengthen them, so that all would know that their strength was entirely from God. Again, these men were to be fathers of the Church and physicians who would heal the weak. But they would be unable to pity the weaknesses of others unless they had first experienced their own weakness.

And so our Lord strengthened these pillars of the world, that is, of the Church. One pillar, Saint Peter, was very weak indeed, to be overthrown by the words of a single maidservant. Afterwards the Lord strengthened this pillar. He did so first when he asked him three times: "Peter, do you love me?" and Peter three times answered, "I love you." For when he had three times denied the Lord, his love for him was to some extent lessened and this pillar became weak and broke, but by three times confessing his love for him it was strengthened. This strengthening was followed by another when the Holy Spirit was sent. Then this pillar became so strong that he could not be moved by being flogged, stoned, threatened, and at last even by being put to death.

Again, that other pillar, Paul, was undoubtedly weak at first, but hear how strong he became afterwards. *I am certain,* he said, *that neither death nor life, nor angels nor anything else in all creation will be able to separate me from the love of God.*

(Sermon 16, 298-301)

Aelred of Rievaulx (1109-1167), a native of Yorkshire, spent part of his youth at the court of King David of Scotland. About the year 1133 he entered the Cistercian monastery of Rievaulx of which he later became abbot. His writings, which combine mystical and speculative theology, earned him the title, "The Bernard of the North." The most important works of this master of the spiritual life are *The Mirror of Charity* and *Spiritual Friendship.*

Transfiguration of the Lord

Gospel: Matthew 17:1-9

This is my beloved Son.

Commentary: Augustine

The Lord Jesus shone like the sun; his garments became as white as snow; and Moses and Elijah were conversing with him. Peter saw this and, taking a human point of view as human beings will, said: *Lord, it is good for us to be here.* He had grown weary of the crowd, he had found solitude on the mountain; there he had Christ as the food of his soul. Why then should he go back down to toil and pain, when here he had a holy love of God and therefore a holy way of life? He wanted this happiness for himself so he continued: *If you are willing, let us set up three tents here: one for you, one for Moses, and one for Elijah.* The Lord gave no reply to this suggestion, yet Peter was answered. For as he was speaking a bright cloud came and overshadowed them. Peter was asking for three tents; the heavenly answer showed us that what the human mind sought to divide is in fact one. The word of God is Christ, the word of God is in the law, the word of God is in the prophets. Why then, Peter, do you seek to divide? You ought rather to combine. You ask for three: understand that the three are one.

As the cloud overshadowed them and became as it were a single tent for them, a voice was heard from the cloud saying: *This is my beloved Son.* Moses was there and Elijah was there, but the voice did not say: These are my beloved sons. For it is one thing to be the only Son, another to be adopted children. He of whom the law and the prophets had boasted was being singled out. *This is my beloved Son in whom I am well pleased; listen to him.* You heard him in the prophets, you heard him in the law; indeed, where have you not heard him? On hearing these words they fell to the ground.

We are already being shown here that the kingdom of God is to be found in the Church. The Lord is here, the law and the prophets are here; but the Lord is here as Lord, while the law is present in the person of Moses and prophecy in the person of Elijah, both of whom are here as servants, as subordinates. They are here as vessels, he as the fountain. Moses and the prophets spoke and wrote; but they were being filled from him when they poured out their message.

The Lord put out his hand and raised up the prostrate men. Then *they saw no one but only Jesus.* The prostration of the disciples signified that we die; for to humans it is said: *You are of the earth, and to the earth you shall return.* Then, when the Lord raised them up he signified the resurrection. After the resurrection will you have any need of the law? Any need of prophecy? Therefore Elijah is no longer to be seen, Moses is no longer to be seen. What is left to you? *In the beginning was the Word, and the Word was with God, and the Word was God.* The Word is left to you *so that God may be all in all.*

Go down, Peter. You longed to take your rest on the mountain, but now the Lord tells you: Go down to work in the world, to serve in the world, to be condemned and crucified in the world. Life came down to be slain; Bread came down to suffer hunger; the Way came down to endure weariness on his journey; the Fountain came down to experience thirst. Do you refuse to work and to suffer? Do not seek your own interests. Practice charity; preach the truth. Then you will attain immortality and find rest.

(Sermon 78, 2.3-6: PL 38, 490.491-492)

Augustine (354-430) was born at Thagaste in Africa and received a Christian education, although he was not baptized until 387. In 391 he was ordained priest and in 395 he became coadjutor bishop to Valerius of Hippo, whom he succeeded in 396. Augustine's theology was formulated in the course of his struggle with three heresies: Manichaeism, Donatism, and Pelagianism. His writings are voluminous and his influence on subsequent theology immense. He molded the thought of the Middle Ages down to the thirteenth century. Yet he was above all a pastor and a great spiritual writer.

Assumption of the Blessed Virgin Mary

Gospel: Luke 9:39-56

The Mighty One has done great things to me and has exalted the humble.

Commentary: Bernard

Today the glorious Virgin has ascended into heaven, surely filling up the measure of joy of those who dwell there. But it might seem more fitting for us to weep than to clap our hands. If heaven rejoices in Mary's presence, does it not follow that our world below should bemoan her absence? Nevertheless, let us make an end of our repining, for here we have no abiding city: we seek the very city to which blessed Mary has gone today. If we are enrolled as citizens of heaven, it is surely right for us to remember her and to share her joy even in our exile, even here beside the waters of Babylon. Our Queen has gone before us, and so glorious has been her entry into paradise that we, her servants, confidently follow our mistress, crying: *Draw us after you and we shall run toward the fragrance of your perfumes.* We in our exile have sent on ahead of us our advocate who, as mother of our judge and mother of mercy, will humbly and effectively look after everything that concerns our salvation.

Today earth has sent a priceless gift up to heaven, so that by giving and receiving within the blessed bond of friendship, the human is wedded to the divine, earth to heaven, the depths to the heights. A sublime fruit of the earth has gone up to heaven, from whence the best gifts, the perfect gifts descend. The blessed Virgin has ascended on high and therefore she too will give gifts to us. And why not? Surely she lacks neither the ability to do so, nor the will. She is the queen of heaven; she is compassionate; she is the mother of the only-begotten Son of God. This more than anything proves the greatness of her power and love— unless, perhaps, we do not believe that the Son of God honors his mother, or unless we doubt that Love itself, which is born of God and rested nine months in her womb, evoked a response of love in her heart.

But quite apart from the benefits that will accrue to us through her glorification, if we love her we shall rejoice because she goes to her Son. We shall certainly congratulate her without reserve, unless—which God forbid—we are wholly without gratitude toward her who has found for us the way of grace. The Lord, whom she first received when he entered the village of this world, today receives her into the holy city. But can you imagine with how much joy, with how much glory? On earth there was no worthier place for Mary to receive the son of God than the temple of her virginal womb. Nor in heaven is there a worthier place for her than that royal throne to which her Son has today exalted her.

Who can describe either how Christ was begotten or how Mary was taken up into heaven? Just as Mary surpassed in grace all others on earth, so also in heaven is her glory unique. If eye has not seen or ear heard or the human heart conceived what God has prepared for those who love him, who can express what he has prepared for the woman who gave him birth and who loved him, as everyone knows, more than anyone else? Blessed indeed is Mary, blessed in many ways, both in receiving the Savior, and in being received by the Savior.

(Sermon 1 on the Assumption of Mary: PL 183, 415-417)

Bernard (1090-1153) entered the monastery of Citeaux with thirty companions in 1112. He received his monastic training under the abbot, Saint Stephen Harding, who sent him in 1115 to make a foundation at Clairvaux in France. Soon one of the most influential religious forces in Europe, Bernard was instrumental in founding the Knights Templar and in the election of Pope Innocent I in 1130. He was a strenuous opponent of writers such as Abelard, Gilbert de la Porree, and Henry of Lausanne. Above all, Bernard was a monk; his sermons and theological writings show an intimate knowledge of Scripture, a fine eloquence, and an extraordinarily sublime mysticism.

Triumph of the Cross

Gospel: John 3:13-17

The Son of Man must be lifted up.

Commentary: Andrew of Crete

The cross is raised and appears above the earth, which until recently malice had kept hidden. It is raised, not to receive glory (for with Christ nailed to it what greater glory could it have?) but to give glory to God who is worshipped on it and proclaimed by it.

It is not surprising that the Church rejoices in the cross of Christ and robes herself in festal raiment, revealing her bridal beauty as she honors this day. Nor is it surprising that this great throng of people has gathered together today to see the cross exposed aloft, and to worship Christ whom they see raised upon it.

For the cross is exposed in order to be raised, and is raised to be exposed. What cross? The cross which a little while ago was hidden in a place called The Skull, but now is everywhere adored. This is what we rejoice over today; this is what we celebrate; this is the point of the present feast; this is the manifestation of the mystery. For this hidden and life-giving cross had to be exposed, set on high like a city on a hill or a lamp on a stand, for all the world to see.

We who worship Christ on the cross must try to grasp the greatness of his power and all the wonders he has wrought through the cross on our behalf; the holy David says: *Our God and eternal King has wrought salvation throughout the world.* For through the cross the nations were caught as in a net and the seeds of faith were sown everywhere. With the cross, as though with a plow, the disciples of Christ cultivated the unfruitful nature of humankind, revealed the Church's ever-green pastures, and gathered in an abundant harvest of believers in Christ. By the cross the martyrs were strengthened, and as they fell they smote down those who struck them. Through the cross

Christ became known, and the Church of the faithful, with the scriptures ever open before her, introduces us to this same Christ, the Son of God, who is truly God and truly Lord, and who cries out: *Any who wish to come after me must deny themselves and take up their cross and follow me.*

(Homily 11 on the Exaltation of the Venerable Cross PG 97, 1036. 1037. 1040-1041. 1044-1045)

Andrew of Crete (c.660-c.720), born in Damascus, became a monk in Jerusalem. He represented his patriarch at the Third Council of Constantinople which condemned the Monothelite heresy in 681. In about 692 he became metropolitan of Crete and in 712, no doubt under pressure from the emperor, took part in the heretical synod in Constantinople which set aside that condemnation, but he soon recanted. He defended the veneration of images under Leo the Isaurian. A remarkable orator, of whose homilies a score have so far been published, and one of the principal hymnographers of the Eastern Church, he is remembered in particular for developing the elaborate hymn known as the canon.

All Saints

Gospel: Matthew 5:1-12

Be glad and rejoice, for your reward will be great in heaven.

Commentary: Gregory Palamas

God is wonderful in his saints. He will give strength and power to his people. Consider the meaning of these prophetic words and try to understand them. The psalm says that God gives strength and power to all his people, for with God there is no partiality; nevertheless it is only in his saints that he fills us with wonder. For just as the sun pours down its rays from above abundantly upon all alike, but only those who have eyes can see them, and then only if their eyes are open, so too does God send down from above his abundant help to all, since he is the source of salvation and light, ever overflowing with mercy and goodness. Yet it is not just anyone who can so benefit from his grace and power as to practice and become perfect in virtue, or even perform miracles, but only those of good disposition, who show their faith in God and their love for him by their actions, who turn away completely from evil, cling steadfastly to God's commandments, and raise the eyes of their minds to Christ, the Sun of Righteousness himself.

Christ not only stretches out his unseen helping hand from heaven to those engaged in the struggle, but he also encourages us in a perceptible way through the gospel words: *Everyone who acknowledges me before other people, I in my turn will acknowledge before my Father in heaven.*

The Church of Christ honors even after their death those who have lived a truly godly life. Every day of the year it commemorates the saints who departed hence on that day, leaving this mortal life. It sets the life of each of them before us for our benefit, and also shows us how each died, whether they fell asleep in peace or ended their lives in martyrdom. On this day, however, the Church gathers them all together and sends up a common hymn in their honor.

My brothers and sisters, let us too honor the saints of God. How shall we honor them? By imitating them, by purifying ourselves from every stain of body and spirit and by ceasing to sin until, by this abstinence, we are brought to a sanctity like theirs. On these festival days at least let us offer God bodies and souls that are acceptable to him, so that we too, by the prayers of the saints, may gain a share in their glory and eternal bliss. May we all attain to this by the grace and mercy of our Lord Jesus Christ, to whom with his eternal Father and the most holy, good, and life-giving Spirit belongs glory now and always and for endless ages. Amen.

(Homily 25: PG 151, 321. 328-329. 332)

Gregory Palamas (1296-1359) was born at Constantinople, and prepared by the piety of his parents for a monastic vocation. At the age of about 20 he became a monk of Mount Athos. In 1347 he was made bishop of Thessalonica. Gregory stressed the biblical teaching that the human body and soul form a single united whole. On this basis he defended the physical exercises used by the Hesychasts in prayer, although he saw these only as a means to an end for those who found them helpful. He followed Saint Basil the Great and Saint Gregory of Nyssa in teaching that although no created intelligence can ever comprehend God in his essence, he can be directly experienced through his uncreated "energies," through which he manifests himself to and is present in the world. God's substance and his energies are distinct from one another, but they are also inseparable. One of these energies is the uncreated divine light, which was seen by the apostles on Mount Tabor. At times this is an inward illumination; at other times it is outwardly manifested.

All Souls

Gospel: Luke 7:11-17

Young man, I say to you, arise.

Commentary: Augustine

It is inevitable that we should be sad when those we love depart from us by dying. Although we know they are not leaving us for ever, that they have but gone a little ahead of us, that we who remain will follow them, nevertheless our nature shrinks from death, and when it takes a loved one we are filled with sorrow simply because of our love for that person. That is why the Apostle did not tell us that we should not be saddened, but that we should not be saddened in the same way as those who have no hope. In the death of those who are close to us we experience both sadness at the necessity of losing them, and hope of getting them back. By the former we are distressed, by the latter consoled; in the one our weakness touches us, in the other faith restores us. In our loss the human condition mourns, but through hope the divine promise heals.

Accordingly, the solemn pomp of the burial rites, the thronging funeral procession, the costly and careful interment, the raising of a rich monument at the grave—all these things are some kind of solace for the living but no help to the dead. However, there is no doubt that the dead are helped by the prayers of holy Church, by the saving sacrifice, and by alms dispensed for their souls; these things are done that they may be more mercifully dealt with by the Lord than their sins deserve. The whole Church observes the custom handed down by our fathers: that those who have died within the fellowship of Christ's body and blood should be prayed for when they are commemorated in their own place at the holy sacrifice, and that we should be reminded that this sacrifice is offered for them as well. When these acts of mercy are solemnly performed for their sake, who can doubt that we are truly giving them our support? The prayers we offer to God for them are not futile. We must not waver in our belief that they are profitable to the dead, to those of the dead at least who have lived in such a way before death that these things can be useful to them afterward. Faithful hearts should be allowed, then, to mourn for their loved ones, but with a grief that can be healed; let them shed over our mortal condition tears that can be wiped away, tears that can be quickly checked by the joy of that faith which assures us that when believers die they go but a little distance from us that they may pass to a better state. Let the loving care of friends be an added consolation, whether it be expended on the funeral rites or devoted to those who grieve. Due attention should be paid to the burial and the construction of tombs for the dead, according to our means, for these are counted as good works in the scriptures. But people whose love for their dead is spiritual as well as physical should pay much greater, more careful and more earnest attention to those things—sacrifices, prayers, and almsgiving—which can assist those who though their bodies may be dead are still alive in spirit.

(Sermon 172, 1-3: PL 38, 936-937)

Augustine (354-430) was born at Thagaste in Africa and received a Christian education, although he was not baptized until 387. In 391 he was ordained priest and in 395 he became coadjutor bishop to Valerius of Hippo, whom he succeeded in 396. Augustine's theology was formulated in the course of his struggle with three heresies: Manichaeism, Donatism, and Pelagianism. His writings are voluminous and his influence on subsequent theology immense. He molded the thought of the Middle Ages down to the thirteenth century. Yet he was above all a pastor and a great spiritual writer.

Dedication
of the Lateran Basilica

Gospel: Luke 19:1-10

Today salvation has come to this house.

Commentary: Thomas of Villanova

D ear brothers and sisters, if we attend faithfully and diligently and
are living holy and upright lives, then whenever we celebrate the
solemnity of an altar or church, the actions done in these temples made
by human hands are fulfilled in us and build us up spiritually. For he
did not lie who said: *The temple of God is holy, and you are that temple.*
When understood spiritually, therefore, this feast is a feast of holy
souls, since they are living temples of the living God.

God is indeed to be worshiped in corporeal things, but what are all
the churches of the world compared with the marvelous, magnificent
and immense creation of his own hands? When Solomon dedicated
his great temple of old, that entire building constructed by craftsmen
seemed mean to him in comparison with the loftiness and expanse of
the heavens; *The heaven of heavens cannot contain you,* he said, *how
much less this house which I have built?*

But the soul is worthier still, more splendid and more capacious
than the heavens, for the entire world cannot fill it. It is made in God's
image, and for this reason the Lord takes his repose in it. Holy souls
are therefore most truly God's holiest temples. That is why the Apostle
says: *Do you not know that you are God's temple and that God's Spirit
dwells in you?* If you do not believe the Apostle, then believe him who
said: *Those who love me will obey my words, and my Father will love
them and we will come to them and make our dwelling in them. I will
dwell in them and walk about in them.*

Great indeed is the capacity of the soul, if there is room in it not
only to dwell but to walk about! What after all are the faculties of

NEW CITY PRESS
202 CARDINAL RD.
HYDE PARK NY 12538

Thank you for choosing this book.
If you would like to receive regular information
about New City Press titles, please fill in this card.

Title purchased: _____

Please check the subjects
that are of particular interest to you:

☐ **FATHERS OF THE CHURCH**

☐ **CLASSICS IN SPIRITUALITY**

☐ **CONTEMPORARY SPIRITUALITY**

☐ **THEOLOGY**

☐ **SCRIPTURE AND COMMENTARIES**

☐ **FAMILY LIFE**

☐ **BIOGRAPHY / HISTORY**

Other subjects of interest: _____

Name: _____

Address: _____

_____

upright souls but broad places wherein God walks? Whenever, then, you feel within yourselves the movements of good desires and dispositions, the pangs of contrition, or the fire of devotion, recognize the steps of God, the signs of the Holy Spirit, as he walks in his temple.

Think, then, dear brothers and sisters, how fearful and anxious the souls of the just should be lest anything base or unbecoming be found in them to offend the eyes of so majestic a God! How carefully they should protect themselves on every side so as not to displease by any wrong thought or desire or action the God who dwells within them! The honor bestowed on them is great, and great should be their fear. It is for this reason that after the Apostle said: *Do you not know that you are God's temple and God's Spirit dwells in you?* He rightly added: *If any violate the temple of God, God will destroy them.* What an insult, what wickedness it would be to drive the Holy Spirit from his dwelling and profane his sanctuaries with unclean desires and pleasures!

God says through the prophet: *Be holy because I, the Lord your God, am holy.* It is as if he were saying: God is holy; therefore let his temple be holy, let the heart be holy, the body holy, speech holy, life holy, manners holy, everything holy! Let no envious thought or worldly desire, no coarse word or impure movement, no unchaste glance or disordered action be found in those who have consecrated themselves to God.

> (Homily on the Dedication of the Church 3-7:
> Opera omnia V [Manila], 515 519)

Thomas of Villanova (1486-1555) abandoned an academic career to become in 1516 an Augustinian friar. In 1533 while provincial he sent friars to the New World. After having declined the see of Granada, he was put under obedience to accept the archbishopric of Valencia which had been so neglected that he was excused from attending the Council of Trent. His time and money were devoted to the poor, the sick, and ransoming captives, so that he was called the Beggar Bishop, father of the poor. His many sermons had an influence on Spanish spiritual literature.

Immaculate Conception

Gospel: Luke 1:26-38

Rejoice, O highly favored daughter, the Lord is with you.

Commentary: Manuel II Palaeolgus

He who had predestined Mary to be his mother filled her with his grace; in fact, he was with her even before she gave birth to him. He was born, as Paul would have said, in his own time, and his body was formed from the blood of the immaculate one; but from the moment when she received the first beginning of her being in the womb of her childless mother, there was never a time when he was not united with her. How could we think otherwise? If John was, as we know, full of the Holy Spirit while still in his mother's womb, how could she fail to be, who was perfect in purity? This is clear from the distinction Gabriel made between present and future when he said: *The Lord is with you.* In answering the immaculate one's question, and trying to explain the manner in which she would conceive, he used the future tense, not the present. He foretold that the all-holy Spirit would come upon her, and the power of the Most High would overshadow her. But in greeting the Virgin, addressing her as favored one, and proclaiming her blessed among women, implying that she surpassed all others in virtue, he was clearly praising her for her present state. He called her favored, not as one who would be, but as one who was already so; and he addressed her as blessed as if to say: Because you are favored, O Virgin, the Lord is with you; and because the Lord is with you, you are blessed among women.

So much for the present. What happened next foretold the future. The consent of the immaculate one was followed by a gift most precious to God, and better than any other that could be offered. For since it was God's secret purpose to recreate and rebuild the universe with a new and surpassing beauty, what could equal a gift which he needed as the very foundation of this secret purpose? The excellence of this gift is obvious to everyone. When Mary made her free offering and uttered her eager prayer for God's will to be done: *I am the handmaid of the Lord; let what you have said be done to me;* at that very moment, by the will of the Father and the cooperation of the Spirit, the Word who is of one nature with them, coeternal, and equally without beginning, was conceived in the Virgin's womb and assumed our nature without pollution. Then, coming forth with his acquired nature, without mingling the natures of created being and the Creator, he appeared as one person. He deified the nature he received, and it acted as a leaven by which he saved the whole of humanity.

(Homily on the Dormition of Mary:
Prochte Orient 16, Fasc. III [1922] 552-553)

Manuel II Palaeologus (1350-1425) was one of the most remarkable writers of the late Byzantine Empire. He became sole emperor on the death of his father in 1391, but following a stroke in 1421 he abdicated and became a monk. His writings include letters, essays, speeches, sermons, apologetics, controversy, and liturgical compositions. His most notable works are a series of twenty-six conferences with a Muslim and a treatise on the procession of the Holy Spirit.

165

Index of Scripture

Index of Authors